RIS K

Volume 1

A fifty-year collection of the very best
funny, risque, and dirty stories ever told!!

Where the comedians of America get their material!!

Your source of stories for your next party!!

Les Davis

American Literary Press, Inc.
Five Star Special Edition
Baltimore, Maryland

RIS Ⓚ

Library of Congress
Cataloging in Publication Data
ISBN 1-56167-401-X

Library of Congress Card Catalog Number:
97-076976

Published by

American Literary Press, Inc.
Five Star Special Edition
8019 Belair Road, Suite 10
Baltimore, Maryland 21236

Manufactured in the United States of America

PREFACE

This book is written for **adults only** and should not be sold to anyone under the age of 18. You have just purchased the greatest collection of funny, risqué stories ever compiled in one volume.

The only purpose of this book (besides making you laugh !) is to provide you and your friends with a seemingly endless source of stories for your next party or get-together.

This collection was compiled over a fifty year period with the sole thought in mind that some day I would publish it for all to enjoy.

Every time I heard a "good story", I would make a special effort to write it down, put it in my billfold and later file it in the "Joke File" when I returned home. I did this faithfully, day in and day out, just like other people work out or spend all their spare time on the golf course.

Just think of the many funny stories you've heard in your lifetime, only to have them go in one ear and out the other , saying to yourself, "Why didn't I write it down so I could remember it ?" Well, if you are like most people, you didn't But I did and that's what makes this book a "One of a kind."

You are about to read the very best in risqué stories, from babies in their cradles to octogenarians; from farmers to business people; from chickens to zebras; and from virtually every kind of living creature (to a few dead ones!) engaged in every kind of activity known to man.

Most of the stories are "quickies" - no long, drawn out, boring speeches that put you to sleep before they ever reach the punch line. Some of the jokes are new and some were not new when Columbus discovered America, but all the jokes will make you smile, and who knows, some will even make you laugh.

WARNING! A few of the jokes in this collection are clean. They have been deliberately inserted so that you may test yourself as to how open-minded a person you are !

Not everyone likes bawdy stories (Abraham Lincoln did !) and others love them. That's what makes this world so interesting. Different strokes for different folks. But **PLEASE KEEP THIS BOOK AWAY FROM CHILDREN** or anyone else whose tastes are different from yours. This book was written for those of you (and there are millions like you) who enjoy this kind of material and who want to howl over these stories along with your friends.

Whenever you want to be the star of your next party, just go through this collection and arm yourself with a few of these stories before you leave home. Enjoy the book, refer to it often, and become an expert at story-telling by committing your favorites to memory.

And remember, wherever you go, put a smile on your face ! You'll be amazed how many doors it will open for you. Best of all, your friends and family will wonder what you've been up to !!

Thank you for purchasing this book and do keep in mind it was written especially for you.

Les Davis
Golden Beach, Florida

ABOUT THE AUTHOR

As a teenager, Les Davis knew what his lifelong hobby was to be : **COLLECTING** - not coins, stamps, or antiques, but humorous stories.

A native of Indiana, Mr. Davis served in World War II as a paratrooper in the Eleventh Airborne Division of the United States Army.

He received his Bachelor of Science degree in Elementary Education from the University of Illinois. However, in his senior year, he was offered a job as an announcer at a local radio station and so fell in love with the work that he gave up his plans to become a teacher and made radio and television his career. During this time, he served in the capacities of announcer and news director for numerous radio and television stations.

In 1956, President Dwight D. Eisenhower founded people-to people International, a non-political, non-profit organization working outside of the governments to advance the cause of world peace through international friendships. The following year Mr. Davis was invited to join this organization as a Delegation Leader for groups of American citizens visiting the then Soviet Union and other countries to promote peace among all peoples. Mr. Davis worked for people-to-people for thirty years.

During his career, Les Davis stuck consistently with his hobby, compiling and filing daily every new and not-so-new funny story he heard or read. This book represents the fruits of a hobby he continues to enjoy to this very day.

Les Davis was listed in <u>Who's Who in America</u> from 1982 through 1986. He is a member of the American Legion, The Veterans of Foreign Wars and the Lions Club.

Upon his retirement in 1987, Mr. Davis began culling from his 55-year collection of some 100,000 stories (from clean to "unwashed"), 4,000 of those he considers his best, a process that took more than nine years to complete.

Mr. Davis and his wife Virginia (who has put many hours into this project, also) have two daughters, five grandchildren, and four great-grandchildren. Mr. And Mrs. Davis divide their living time between Golden Beach, Florida and Winnebago, Illinois.

Dear Reader:

You will note that each joke or story in this book has been numbered so that you will be able to find your favorites quickly. Just jot down the number of the ones you especially want to remember so that you can refer to them when you have guests in or are going out to a party or reception. This page and the following page have been left blank solely for this purpose.

P.S. You know, all of us have heard and remembered two or three favorite risqué stories in our lifetime. Why not write them down and send them to **RISQUE PUBLISHING COMPANY, P.O. BOX 32, WINNEBAGO, ILLINOIS, 61088.** We will be happy to send you **$5.00** for each of your stories that we use in the second edition and we'll make sure your name is in the book as the contributor! Start thinking about the funniest stories you have ever heard and **DO IT NOW !**

(1)

Wives, at your next party sing this to your friends…… Oh how we danced on the night we were wed. If you think we danced, you've got rocks in your head !

(2)

THE PERFECT GIRL…… She doesn't wink, she doesn't flirt, she tells no gossip, spreads no dirt, she has no line, she plays no tricks, but …… give her time…… she's only six.

(3)

JUST WAIT TILL YOU GET OLD…….We're well aware our youth has been spent, that our get-up and go has got up and went; but we don't mind, as we think with a grin, of all the great places our get-up has been.

(4)

DEAR LOVE ADVISOR, Tonight he popped the question, My answer was "YES" MY question is ……. "Do you still think he will ask me to marry him ?"

(5)

Have you heard about the new disease that is prevalent in men over 50 ? its called "cabbage fever"……The stalk won't support the head.

(6)

It has happened to your wife…My feet went up in the air… My face turned crimson red I felt both cold and wet, I wished that I were dead. Now the moral of the story……Is never sit, abrupt…… always look behind you… The seat may still be up.

(7)

The young kid was talking to his younger brother. "How's your memory, how far can you remember back?" The older brother replied, "Oh, I can remember way back to when our Mom and Pop got married. The younger brother came back with, "By God you should, you were nine years old at the time!"

(8)

They have invented a new cocktail down at the Peacock Lounge. It's made with equal parts of Bourbon, Spanish Fly and Ex-Lax...... All you have to do is drink three of them and I guarantee you won't know whether your coming or going.

(9)

You've heard of the young man from Kent whose thing was so bent...... To save a lot of trouble, he put it in double and instead of coming , he went.

(10)

What are the three words you dread most while having sex ? "Honey, I'm home."

(11)

A guy sees an ad in the paper -SAFE SEX- Arch Street. So the guy goes there and a nun answers the door. He hands her the money and the nun motions toward a door. He goes through it and finds himself in the street. He looks back and the sign says: YOU HAVE JUST BEEN SCREWED BY THE SISTERS OF MERCY.

(12)

The housewife was telling her neighbor, "My husband's really pissed at me. He was rummaging around in the bathroom and found my birth control pills." The neighbor said, "So what ? The housewife answered, "He had a vasectomy three years ago !"

(13)

Why is making love in a canoe like lite beer ? They're both dam close to water.

(14)

How are men and a place to park your car alike ? The good ones are taken and the only ones left are handicapped !

(15)

"Hey Millie, what's going on ? Where's Fred" "My husband ran off with my best friend," she replied. "Who was it ?" "I don't know, but she's my best friend."

(16)

What's a sure fire way to piss off your husband while your having sex ? Call him up and tell him how good it feels.

(17)

"Hey, honey," said the husband. "the elevator man tells that the guy in 6B has screwed every woman in the building except one." "Yeah," She replied, "Its that snotty Mrs. Baxter on the tenth floor."

"Look at this," says one bar customer to another, holding up his drink, "an ice cube with a hole in it." "Big deal," yawns the second drinker. "I'm married to one."

You know, if it wasn't the hen or the egg that came first...... it had to be the rooster!

The teen age girl told her mother, "Everywhere I go they keep using the word "Virgin". It's virgin this and virgin that. What do I have to do to be a virgin ?"

NEW WORDS TO A OLD SONG: I'm a little sexpot, short and stout, here is my handle and here is my spout. When you turn me on, here's what I shout...... "Sock it to me, baby, let it all hang out!"

A COMPLAINT FOR THE CONDOM FACTORY: Dear Mr. Trojan, My girl friend is pregnant. Your written instructions said, "Put it on my organ". Well having no organ, I put it on my harmonica.

SIGN IN THE OLD FOLKS RESTROOM: " Here I hang, Plum dejected; Want to bang, but ain't erected."

(24)

The old man was always chasing young girls but his wife didn't care. She said, "Dogs are always chasing cars, but if they ever catch one, they can't drive."

(25)

You know, the best way for a wife to get her husband to give up golf is to grab his club at least twice a day.

(26)

And, remember this, in the game of love we claim there'd be only one reward….. It isn't how you played the game but how often you have scored !

(27)

The young lady lying in bed with the 70 year old gentleman was really disgusted. She said to her bed partner, "Honey, do you think the Star Spangled Banner would help"

(28)

Little Willie lost his dog and went all over town asking people to help him find it. It's named "Ohio" and it's got a little round "O" right under his tail."

(29)

Confucius say: Man who stick hand down girl's dress usually will get a bust in the mouth !

(30)

A middle aged couple is at the zoo, checking out the gorilla. Meantime, the gorilla is checking out the woman, who happens to have a terrific body. Suddenly, the horny ape smashes a gate, grabs the woman and throws her to the ground. "What should I do ?" screams the woman. "Do what you do to me !" her husband yells back. "Tell him you have a headache !"

(31)

A cook who boils carrots and peas in the same pot will ruin the whole meal.

(32)

Which is more profitable, a one story whore house or a two story whore house ? One story, of course ' cause there ain't no damn overhead.

(33)

A drunk walks into a catholic church and slips into the confessional. The priest, seeing him, comes down the aisle, enters the other side of the box and asks, "How may I help you, my son ? And the drunk says, "if there's toilet paper on your side, will you slip me some ?"

(34)

If your American when you go to the bathroom, what are you while your in there ? European.

(35)

Hung over on the morning after the office Christmas party, the guy asks his wife, "Did I do anything stupid last night ?" She says, "you sure did. You tried to screw the boss's girlfriend and he fired you!" " yeah ?" the guy rages. "Well, screw him!" "I did," says the wife. "your rehired."

(36)

Then there was a 90 year old guy arrested for rape. He won the case. The evidence wouldn't stand up in court.

(37)

Why is laying a guy for the first time like a snowstorm ? You don't know how many inches your going to get, or how long it'll last !

(38)

Did you hear about the pitcher who caught a line drive on the fly ? It ruined his sex life.

(39)

Did you hear about the rooster who got caught in a rainstorm ? He made a duck under the barn !

(40)

Dumb Dotty thought Peter Pan was the wash basin in the little boy's room !

(41)

The Cheerleaders at little Norfolk, Virginia College came up with a new cheer and it went like this: Rah, Rah Rah! WE DON'T SMOKE ! WE DON'T DRINK ! NORFOLK, NORFOLK, WIN, WIN, WIN !

(42)

In Illinois, when an old guy goes out with a fifteen year old girl, they call him "Romeo" but he spends 10 years in Juliet !

(43)

The old maid found a tramp under her bed and her stomach was on the bum all the rest of the night !

(44)

Do you know what MISERY IS ? It's when you are billing and cooing with your boyfriend and suddenly you recognize your husbands voice in the booth behind you !

(45)

What did the golf ball say to the baseball ? "You may make a home run at times, but I'm the one that always gets in the hole !

(46)

A cute coed was asked how she made out the morning after the wedding to a rich 72 year old man ? her answer was, " Did you ever try to put a oyster in a piggy bank ?"

(47)

Know what a "TEASER" is ? It's a girl who builds the bonfire, then goes home when it's time to toast marshmallows !

(48)

NOW , LETS TEST YOUR IQ: Which word is out of place here ? RUG, EGG, SEX, WIFE ? it's obvious, you can beat the other three, but you can't beat sex ……….

(49)

There is only thing that makes a man marry a woman ….. that thing is the thing she won't let him have any other way……..

(50)

How many vitamins and calcium is there in a KISS ? …. Enough to make a bone about six inches long.

(51)

Do you know why they have never taught Donkeys how to talk ? ….Nobody likes a smart ass !

(52)

Did you hear about the farmer who crossed a hen with a porcupine ? We don't know what he got, but when it lays an egg, everybody in town can hear it scream.

(53)

You fellows who gave up smoking are always the ones who are trying to get their hands on a hot butt.

(54)

Two lady neighbors talking over the back fence and one says' "I'm really mad at you !" "WHY" the other one replied. "I understand that you have been going around telling all our other neighbors that my husband has a wart on the end of his thing !" the other lady said, " I did not... I only said it FELT like it !"

(55)

You know the Peacock Lounge has a great bartender. He makes a martini that is SO STRONG it comes with an olive, a twist of lemon and a warning on the glass directed to denture- wearers !

(56)

Why don't teenagers clean up their rooms ? I can't tell you what my sons room looks like but it was the first time I ever saw a roach running with one leg over it's eyes !

(57)

Speaking of kids, don't you wish the school bus went only one way ?

(58)

I really haven't been getting any sleep lately. The couple next door are newlyweds and every night this week they were in the shower together. The least they could do is turn on the water !

OK , what's six inches long, has a head on it and when a guy puts his hand in his pocket, he can feel it ?   You are absolutely right ……. It's American currency !

WONDER WHAT THIS MEANS ? Ad in a local paper under "Real Estate" GET A LOT WHILE YOU ARE YOUNG !

REMEMBER GIRLS : Never marry a man who snores…but, most important, be very careful how you find out !

If you don't know the difference between a man and a shower, you had better find out before you get under one !

UNCLE HOMER was cleaning out the old outside privy with gasoline, and, like the dummy he was, lit his pipe and blew himself and the outhouse over a 100 yards into the pasture. AUNT HELEN came running out and hollered, "My God Homer, I bet your sure glad you didn't let that one in the house !"

Two drunks at the bar and one says to the other, "My good friend Paul is getting married in two weeks, what do you say we give his bride a shower ?" The other drunk replied, "That's a great idea and you can count on me to bring the soap !"

As the guy checked out of his motel room, he told the manager, "I've got a real complaint this morning, I didn't get a bit of sleep last night, the woman in the next room was eating candy all night long and she kept screaming, "OH HENRY ! OH HENRY!

Then there was the Chinese couple who went to court to have their teenage virgin daughters names changed. They want to name them TU YUNG TO, TO DUM TO and NO YEN TO !

Did you hear about the poor mistreated parakeet ? His owner made him kiss a cockatoo every day !

Of all the birdies in the sky, I'd rather be a duck; I'd fly along the beaches low and watch the people….. holding hands !

Did you hear about the old geezer who died while a young nurse was massaging his "talleywhacker" ? The death certificate read, "Cause of death …… STROKE !"

Why is 68 the speed limit for women when they are in bed ? At 69 she blows a rod.

(71)

What is the difference between a proctologist and a bartender ?   The proctologist only has to deal with one butt hole at a time !

(72)

Two old geezers are sitting on the front porch visiting when a old hound dog comes up on the porch, lies down and starts licking between his legs. One old man studied for a while and said, "Well look at that, Boy, oh Boy, I sure wished I could do that ! His friend replied, "Go ahead if you want to, but I do think you ought to pet him first".

(73)

Did you ever wonder why the government doesn't tax your penis ? I guess it's because 90 % of the time it's inactive. 10% of the time it is in the hole. It's got two dependents and both of them are nuts !

(74)

A lady walks into a bar with a duck under her arm. Bartender looks up and asks, "Where in the hell did you get that pig ?" The woman replied, "Dummy, What's wrong with you, that's not a pig, it's a duck !" The bartender says, "shut up, I was talking to the duck !

(75)

Do you know how to tell when you are getting old ? It's when you spend all night in bed with a woman, dawn comes and you don't !

(76)

What's six inches long and all women love it ? A dollar bill.

(77)

What's six inches long, has a bald head on it and drives a woman crazy ? A 100 dollar bill.

(78)

It was weeks before he got up the courage to engage his girlfriend in heavy petting. He had a small penis and was so embarrassed by it, he had to wait until they were in a very dark place, then pulled it out and placed it gingerly in her hand. "No thanks" she replied. " I don't smoke."

(79)

I've got a great idea, said the wife to her husband, "What do you say we go out tonight and really have a good time ?" "suits me " the husband replied, "if you get home before I do , DON'T FORGET TO LEAVE THE LIGHTS ON IN THE HALLWAY ! "

(80)

The rural minister was lecturing the Sunday School boys and girls on the nature of sins and damnation. He asked one boy, "Do you know where little boys and girls go when they do bad things ?" "yes, sir," replied the boy, "Back of the haystack behind the dairy barn."

(81)

Do you know what a "Mourner" is ? It's the same as a "Nooner" but only sooner !

(82)

HERE'S A TOAST JUST FOR HUSBAND AND WIFE: May you live as long as you want to and want to as long as you live. If I'm asleep and you want to, wake me. If I'm awake and don't want to, make me !

(83)

NOW A TOAST FOR YOUR FAVORITE BARTENDER: The evening sum can kiss the sky and a man can kiss his wife goodbye. The morning dew can kiss the grass and you, my dear friend, can fill my glass ! (Don't even think about using another word !)

(84)

DO YOU MEN KNOW WHAT HENPECKED IS ? It's a husband that forgot to tell his pregnant wife that he was sterile.

(85)

The little five-year-old boy was telling his playmate, "Papa and Momma must have had a bird loose in their bedroom last night " I heard Papa say, "Shall I let it fly, or catch it in a towel ?"

(86)

That same little boy went to his Daddy the next day and asked, "Daddy, are window shades good to eat ?" "Why would you ask such a question Son, replied the father ? "Because" , the little boy said. "I heard Mommy tell the milk man to pull down the shade and he could tear off a piece !"

(87)

A guy walked into the newspaper office and said, "I want to put an ad in the personals so my dog will see it and come home." The classified clerk replied, "Come on mister, you're pulling my leg !" "Dogs can't read !" The man sighed and said "The one I'm married to can !"

(88)

The little five year old boy told his Dad, "I asked Mama where I came from, and she told me. Dad replied, "What did she tell you Son ?" The little boy came back with, "Mama said I was so sweet, I came from a sugar bowl." Dad said, "Well son, that's about the size of it !"

(89)

Yes still another toast: Here's to the couple on the cot, it must be long for she's getting a lot, what they are talking about will never be read, …… but what they are making will have to be fed !

(90)

Did you hear about Tom, Dick and Harry ? His mother made him stop !

(91)

Do you know what a "suburb" is ? It's a small community where you can borrow a man's wife but you can not borrow his golf clubs !

(92)

The Highway patrolman stopped a speeding car and noticed the driver was bombed out of his mind. The patrolman gave him a stern warning and went on to say, "Do you realize you were going over 70 miles per hour ?" The drunk looked at the officer and replied, "I know how fast I was going damn it, I was just trying to hurry home before I had an accident !"

(93)

Here's to the bee who stung the mule ...... and started him to bucking. The same little bee stung Adam and Eve... and started them to ..... eating an apple !

(94)

And then there was the poor little midget who went to a TWIST PARTY in a nudist colony. Somebody put on a hot and fast rock and roll record and the poor little midget almost got clubbed to death !

(95)

Sign over the stool in the men's room: Tinkle, tinkle little star.... In the restroom of the bar. High above the toilet seat.... Please hit the bowl and not your feet !

(96)

A 90 year old man announces his intention to marry a woman of 30. He is persuaded to have a medical exam first. "Everyone tell me I need a checkup to see if I'm sexually fit," he says to the doctor. "O.K." says the medic, "Let see your sex organs." So the old guy sticks out his tongue and his middle finger !

(97)

A 90 year old man marries a women young enough to be his granddaughter. After a week's honeymoon, a friend asks him how things went. "Wonderful," says the ancient groom. "We did it every night." "Are you kidding ?" sputters the friend "At your age ?" "Certainly !" says the groom. "We almost did it Monday night, we almost did it Tuesday night, we..............."

(98)

How come your boss is just like a diaper ? He's always on your ass and he's usually full of crap.

(99)

First slob: "I keep knocking up my girlfriend and yet your girl never gets pregnant. What does she use ?" Second slob: "Listerine." First slob: "But isn't that mouthwash ?" Second slob: "Right."

(100)

A man complains to a doctor of no sex drive and is given a fast acting medicine. Next day the doctor asks, "How was it ?" "Well, good and bad. I took the pill just before dinner, and half-way through the meal I had this great urge, so I threw the food on the floor and screwed my wife right on the table." "Sounds fantastic ! So what's bad ?" "We can't eat at Burger King any more ."

(101)

She buried six husbands and countless lovers and finally she was being buried herself. At the funeral, one mourner says to another, "At long last they're together again." "Which husband do you mean ?" asks the other "None of them I'm talking about her legs."

(102)

A guy is trying to make time with his girl in her living room, but he keeps farting. At each blast, the girl looks at her dog under the sofa and says, "Barney! Come out from there!" Finally, the guy lets loose with an ear-splitting fart. The girl jumps up and yells, "Barney! Get out from there quick before he craps all over you!

(103)

What do you have when you've got two big green balls in your hands? The Jolly Green Giant's undivided attention.

(104)

What's the difference between a good nurse and a real good nurse? A good nurse can make a bed without disturbing the patient. A real good nurse can make a patient without disturbing the bed.

(105)

Two dogs are humping away and a little kid asks his father for an explanation. "Well," the man bluffs, "One dog is very sick and the other is helping carry him to the dog doctor." "Son of a bitch!" says the kid. "Every time you try to help somebody out you wind up getting screwed in the ass."

(106)

One of the great mysteries of life is how the idiot that your daughter married can be the father of the smartest grandchildren in the whole world.

(107)

How about the two roosters who were caught in a downpour ? One ran for the barn, the other made a duck under the porch.

(108)

The wealthy farmer brings three young men to bessie, his prize cow, draws up a stool and says, "Whoever can screw bessie the longest is the man for my beautiful daughter." The first guy shoots off in about a minute. The second manages to last almost twenty minutes. The third screws the cow for nearly three hours. "My daughter's yours," the farmer says. "Tell your daughter to screw herself," says the lucky man. "How much do you want for bessie?"

(109)

God wants to check on his creation, so he calls down to Adam: "HOW'S IT GOING?" "FINE, GOD." "WHAT'S EVE UP TO?" "SHE'S TAKING A BATH IN THE RIVER, GOD." "OH, SHIT- NOW I BET THE FISH WILL ALL SMELL LIKE THAT!"

(110)

Why did the Greek boy leave home ? He didn't like the way he was being reared. And why did he come back ? He couldn't bear to leave his brother's behind.

(111)

Leroy takes Sapphire driving and stops in lovers' lane. He unbuckles his belt and asks, "Honey, is you goin' to be a Chesterfield, what satisfies, or a Camel smoker, what walks a mile ?" "dat depends," breathes Sapphire, reaching for his zipper "on whether you is regular or king size."

(112)

What's the difference between a light bulb and a two-seat sports car ? It's easy to screw in a light bulb.

(113)

Once there was a little girl who swallowed a pin. She didn't feel a prick until she was 17.

(114)

A guy finds a strange - looking old lamp. He rubs it. A genie appears. "You've got one wish." The genie offers. "What'll it be ?" The guy thinks a second and says, "I'd like a Wang that'll touch the ground." All of a sudden his legs fall off!

(115)

The story of the aging: At first, you do it all night long. Then it takes you all night long to do it. And finally, you just long to do it.

(116)

"Do you know the difference between a Dick and a BLT ?" "Nope." "good. Wanna come to my house for lunch ?"

(117)

Autobiography of a homosexual: I've never hugged a parrot, but I've kissed a cockatoo.

(118)

What do you get if you cross a rooster with a telephone pole ? A 30 foot cock that wants to reach out and touch someone.

(119)

Always remember the wisdom of the ancient Chinese playboy: "Fellow who lose key to girl's apartment, get no new key."

(120)

The three biggest lies: "The check is in the mail." I'm from the government and I'm here to help you." "Don't worry, I won't come !"

(121)

Hey Guys, if at first you don't succeed, she's just testing you to see if you need it bad enough to ask her again. Now, you can't blame the girl for waiting 'till you are really hard up. She wouldn't have any fun if you didn't give her a hard time !

(122)

The spelling teacher asked Johnny to use a sentence with the word "EMBARRASSED" in it. Johnny thought for a minute and responded, "I peaked in my sister's bedroom and there was her boyfriend. I saw "EMBARRASSED."

(123)

The young stud told his girlfriend, "Now that we've done what I really like best, isn't there something I can do for you that will make you even more happy ? She replied, "Well, come to think about it, would you please "COME AGAIN!"

(124)

THE CONGRESSMAN'S SECRETARY WROTE THE I.R.S.... I'm filling out my tax form and my name is Jill, is it all right if I deduct the cost of my birth control pill ? Since it's not for enjoyment but to make sure my job is secure on Capital Hill !

(125)

A salesman traveling through a rural area ran over a rooster. He stopped and walked up to the farm house and told the wife, "I'm so sorry, I just ran over your rooster, can I replace him ?" The farm wife replied, "I don't see why not, the chicken's are out behind the barn !"

(126)

Helen Patricia was standing in the hallway twisting and turning, clutching her crotch and looking like she was in sheer misery. One of her friends asked, "You don't look good, are you sick ?" Helen Patricia replied, "No, I have a weight problem .... Somebody's using that damn bathroom and I can't wait another second !"

(127)

Brides, forget about that old saying about something old and something new. What your new husband wants to know, are you going to screw ?

(128)

When you are a guest at a party and see someone you know, you should always ask, "Whom did you bring with you ?" Not, "Who did you come with ?

(129)

Homer was playing golf with his wife, Helen Patricia and , of course, he was really taking a beating. Helen Patricia said, "That's all right honey, cheer up, tonight when we go to bed , you'll know which club to use !" Homer whimpered, "Yes, but damn it, it will be your hole !"

(130)

You know, it is really not surprising that most babies are born at night. That's usually when the nine months are up !

(131)

We asked the old man how he was doing and he replied, "My bats too shaky to get to first base but I'm still in there pitching !"

(132)

Did you hear about the social worker who found that one of her clients was pregnant again ? "This is your seventh baby and you tell me they are all by the same man." "For God sake, why don't you marry him ?" The lady on welfare replied, "Well, frankly ma'am he just isn't my type!"

(133)

Then there was the one about the cop on the beat who noticed a young lad standing in front of the House of Pleasure ! "You're not thinking of going in that house, are you ?" The kid answered, "No officer, I'm just waiting for my daddy to come out !"

(134)

On their 25th wedding anniversary, the husband woke up crying his eyes out and his wife wanted to know what was the matter. He replied, "Do you remember your dad caught us behind the house and he told me if I didn't marry you, he would have me arrested and I would spend 25 years in prison ? Just think..... today I would be a free man !"

(135)

On the morning after their wedding night, the groom got up, went over to the window and said, "gee, it sure is beautiful out !" His new bride replied "Yes, honey, I'm sure it is but, you know something, it would feel a lot better in !"

(136)

NEW BUMPER STICKER: "SUPPORT MENTAL HEALTH OR I'LL KILL YOU"

(137)

The wife says to her husband, "Honey will you please put it in the hole and work it up and down. Maybe, after a while you can get that damn commode working again !"

(138)

Two guys getting loaded in their home bar when the door bell rings and one of them goes to the door. He yells back, "Hey buddy, there's a woman peddler at the door !" His friend replied, "Great .... tell him we'll take two !"

(139)

HERE'S A TOAST TO THE BRIDE AND GROOM: The vows have been said......The cake has been cut.......Let's all hope the bride don't get a big butt !

(140)

A NOTE TO MY WIFE .....I don't need a clock with a buzzer or chime ..... Just play with my stock and I'll get up in time !

(141)

You know fellows there's one thing worse than forgetting to take Vaseline on your honeymoon, and that's finding out you don't need it!

(142)

The senator's secretary asked her boss, "What are you going to do about the Abortion Bill ?" He answered, "Well...if you're sure that's what you want to do........ I'll pay for it !"

(143)

The family doctor told the cute little teenager, "I have good news and bad news. First the good news....You can stop worrying about some boy knocking you up. And now the bad news......one already did !

(144)

The new daddy held his 4 year old son up to see his brand new baby sister through the hospital's viewing window. Inside the window were ten filled cribs plus two empty cribs. "Oh, look daddy, " screamed the four year old. "They've got two more traps set !"

(145)

Do you know what "FRUSTRATED" IS ? It's when you're in a motel room, socking it to your favorite girlfriend and you hear a voice in the next room say, "See, I told you, he wouldn't notice we put pin holes in his condoms !"

(146)

The cute little congressional Page Girl told the senator, "As I promised you, I don't charge for my services, but before you go, perhaps you might be interested in this video tape we just made together !"

(147)

The 98 year-old drunk told a hippie in a bar, "I'm sorry buddy, I didn't mean any offense when I called you a bastard. Why, I've known you since way before your momma married your poppa !"

(148)

Mike Casey asked his new secretary, "Do you know the difference between intercourse and conversation ?" She replied, "Gosh, I guess I really don't know !" Mike said, "Would you mind stepping into my office, I'd like to talk to you !"

(149)

You're on vacation and you've been driving for 10 hours when you come to a nice motel and read the big sign out front, "No vacancy, you dum, dum! Don't you wish you had stopped back there where your wife wanted you to ?"

I wouldn't say she was dumb, but she was invited to her best friends wedding shower and the invitation stated, "BRING YOUR OWN LIQUOR." You won't believe it ..... but she brought her boyfriend !

EVERY HOSPITAL IN THE COUNTRY HAS ONE, SOME CALL HER THE "HEAD NURSE !"   The younger nurses call her "PUBLIC ENEMA NUMBER ONE !"

You know, pigeons are almost human ! They accept the crumbs you throw at them and then turn around and crap all over you !

The fellow came into the bar crying his eyes out. The bartender asked, "What is wrong, buddy ?" The man said, "my wife gave me a whole year's supply of condoms for my birthday and that damn grandson of mine stole both of them !"

Did you hear about the cute little coed and her boyfriend walking in the park ? A pigeon flew over, and do you know what happened, it hit her right on the forehead. Embarrassed, she turned to her boyfriend and asked for a piece of toilet paper. He replied, "What the hell do you want with a piece of toilet paper ? That damn bird's probably a half a mile away by now !"

(155)

The gynecologist had the woman on the table and in stirrups. "My, you have a large cavity down there…..My, you have a large cavity down there !" The lady turned red and really let the doctor have it. She said, "Doctor I know it's big but damn it, you didn't have to say it twice." The Doctor replied, " I didn't say it twice, the second time you heard, it had to be an echo !"

(156)

Do you know what embarrassment is ? It's the first time your wife is wearing her new see-through blouse and two teenagers walk up to you and say, "Are two guys brothers ?"

(157)

The old maid was talking to her friend, " I wouldn't say I was ugly as a child but dirty old men used to give me candy if I wouldn't get into their cars."

(158)

If you love to go camping, here is a tip for you.. "It's a lot easier to get into a sleeping bag if you wake her up first."

(159)

You know, the girls who work as airline stewardesses are the meanest people on earth ! They walk up to you and say, "Is there something you want ?" Then they strap you in the seat !

(160)

Have you heard about the new potent laxative pills they have come up with ? The label warns, "Quick acting, take only one with a glass of water." If you happen to be on the phone, for Gods sake, don't let the party on the other end put you on HOLD !

(161)

Halfway to the office, the business man noticed his socks didn't match so he turned around and headed back home to change them. When he got inside, he could see his wife's bare butt bending over the bathtub. He tiptoed up close, patted little bottom and whispered, "HOW MUCH TODAY, BABY ?" Without even looking up she replied, "Same as always...two quarts of milk and a pound of butter !"

(162)

The sweet, young lady on the cross town bus was cuddling a little poodle in her arms. Every once in a while, she would kiss the puppy and snuggle it up to her breasts. The driver, looking through his mirror said, "Gosh, I sure wish I could change places with that dog." The young lady laughed and said, "Man, you would really be making a big mistake.... We're on our way to the vet to have him castrated !"

(163)

Confucius say: Careless chick who lays down is looking for trouble, usually gets a belly full.

(164)

DID YOU KNOW ? A man's body contains 206 bones, and the one you're thinking about isn't one of them !

(165)

WANT TO HAVE SOME FUN ? The next time you encounter a bachelor buddy who has one if those horrible hangovers shake his hand and tell him, "Congratulations 'ol buddy, that was quite a piece of tail you married last night !"

(166)

WHAT IS A MEAN S.O.B. ? It's a bachelor who invites all his friends over to have sex with his girlfriend the night after the condom broke !

(167)

Did you hear the one about the guy who rushed into the bar and told the bartender, "The drinks are on me !" "My wife ran away with my best friend." The bartender smiled and said, "That's a shame, how come you aren't unhappy ?" "Hell no, I'm not unhappy," replied the guy, "They saved me a fortune.....both of them were pregnant !"

(168)

A pregnant woman was ready to have twins, but the first twin would not push out, his womb mate pushed and pushed but the baby wouldn't budge. Finally, the one trying to get out bawled, "You're blocking my way. Can't you crawl through the bushes." The other baby replied, "There ain't no way I'm going to move, I'm scared to death, it was just last night I saw a big ol' copperhead snake stick it's head in here and how do I know he's not waiting for me when I go out ?"

(169)

The police man stopped a speeding car and asked the lady driver "Where do you think you're going ?" She answered, "To your bedroom, I hope….If I get one more ticket, I'll be riding a bicycle !"

(170)

The honeymooners spent their first days together in a travel trailer. To insure they wouldn't be bothered when they stopped, they put a sign on the door which read, "IF THIS TRAILER STARTS ROCKING, PLEASE DON'T COME KNOCKING !"

(171)

Did you know your neighbor has left her husband because, she said, "He was getting indifferent.." What she meant was…."In different women every night !"

(172)

You can really have your feelings hurt if the answers to the following questions are negative: 1. Do I get the loan. 2. Did I pass my physical 3. How about going to bed with me   4. Was I good.

(173)

Students at the University of Kansas like to tell of the pranks they play on their football rivals, the University of Nebraska. One Saturday morning the Jayhawks went into every stadium restroom and put a sign right above the toilet paper. It read, "University of Nebraska diplomas……take one !"

(174)

The next time you go to a party or reception, get on the microphone and say this……"All of you here who believe in fairies, please raise your hand !" Then say, "All of you who don't believe in fairies better take a good close look at the guy sitting next to you !"

(175)

Salesman Sammy sat down on the train with this gorgeous hunk of women. He offered her cigarette. She smiled. "I don't smoke, but I do hope you will. Smokers give my daddy's business a lot of money." Sammy asked, "I bet your dad is a manufacture of matches ?" "Oh' no sir," she said ." "He's a mortician !"

(176)

The father cornered his teenage son, "OK, where did you take the car last night ?" The boy replied, "Nowhere special….A guy and I just rode around town and stopped at a drive-in !" Dad said, "Well, next time you see that boy….you tell him I found his bra in the back seat !"

(177)

Poor grandpa, he is at the awkward age. If he pumps too slow, he doesn't stay stiff enough and if he pumps too fast, he looses his breath !

(178)

So you want to write a letter but your pen is bone dry. It's sort of a lowdown feeling that can make a strong man cry. First you tap it, then you shake it , but it ain't a bit of use. No matter how you whack the thing, it's out of fucking juice. It's all so frustrating and it ain't no use to try, she won't never get your message if your BALL POINT PEN IS DRY !

(179)

"My what a lovely coat," said the high class lady to her bridge partner, "It must have cost a fortune." Her partner smiled, "No, only one kiss." The high class lady asked suspiciously. "A kiss you gave your husband ?" Her partner answered, "No, the one he gave the maid !"

(180)

And then there was the one about the lady who went to the store to pick up her husband's razor which had been left for repairs. She asked the clerk, "Do you have a razor for Harry Peters ?" The clerk answered, "No ma'am, but we do have one that shaves under your arms !"

(181)

You know, it's easy to grin if you're neat as a pin and gals give you all they've got. But the man worth while is the man who can smile, as his shorts creep up in his crouch !

(182)

LETTER TO THE LOVE ADVISOR: I love my husband so very much but our sex life is really crappy. What can I do to solve the problem ? Signed Mrs. Backhoe. Dear Mrs. Backhoe: If your sex life is as crappy as you say, you have to be doing it wrong !

(183)

This drunk was really teed-off as he staggered into the Peacock Lounge and demanded, "Bartender, have you been shacking up with my wife ?" The bartender lied as he said, "No Sir, of course not !" The drunk replied, "Why don't you try it sometime…then you will understand why I drink so much !"

(184)

Another drunk moved up to this cute model at the bar and said, "How about some, baby ?" She replied, "I'm sorry, I don't give it away, but my friend Helen Hunt does. So, if you're looking for a free lay, you'll just have to go to Helen Hunt for it !"

(185)

A man at the supermarket walked up to the checkout counter with two onions. The girl weighted them and announced, "That will be 89 cents for each onion." The man's face turned red and he replied, "Eighty nine cents for two little onions ?" "You know what you can do with them, don't you ?" The girl looked him square in the eye and said, " Oh mister, I couldn't do that, I already have a two dollar and fifty cent cucumber up there already !"

(186)

Do you understand all this talk about planned parenthood ? You tell me now, how in the hell can anyone plan who their parents are going to be !???

(187)

She was red hot.... But he was not. Her body shook as if in grief, she wept, "I must have some relief !" We are betting that you think she meant a man; instead, all she said was "Turn on the fan."

(188)

The local druggist knew the honeymoon was over when the bride and the groom came into the store and asked, "Can we swap the rest of this Vaseline for a bottle of Alum ?"

(189)

A hitch hiker was exposing his thumb alongside the highway. A sultry she-driver stopped and said, "Slip inside," He slid in beside her and politely inquired, "Want to screw" She replied , "Not here. It's too public," and drove until they reached the forest. He smiled, "Are we going to fuck now ?" She answered, "Not now. Someone might see us," and continued into the woods. As the trees grew denser, the hiker kept repeating his question. But each time she would say, "Not yet we're likely to be seen." Finally she pulled into a deep thicket. He moaned, "Is it sex time NOW ?" She whispered, "Yes, but keep your voice down.....my husband's asleep in the back seat."

(190)

You want to have some fun ? Play this game the next time you have friends in ! Tell your victim, "Let's play a game. Whatever color I say I am. You say you're the same thing with a "E" sound on the end: I am Brown." Your sucker should answer , I'm brownie." "I am Green." " I am Greenie."   "I am Pink." "I am Pinkie." "I am Red." "I am ready." So then you shout: "So am I .... Let's get with it !"

(191)

Before turning your kids loose on the world, teach them your whole name ! A smart tot on a TV show was asked, "Who is your Daddy ?"   Never having heard him called anything but Daddy, the child replied, "Your guess is as good as mine."

(192)

A well dressed gent stumbled into the Peacock Lounge and ordered, "Pour me a stiff one, I've just become the father of twins."   The bartender smiled , "Congratulations ! I'll bet your wife is excited." The man growled, "She will be if she finds out.....she's been looking for grounds to divorce me "

(193)

A lady noticed that her neighbor's children always left one brother out of their games. So she collared one of the other kids and asked, "How come you never let Sammy play ?" The lad retorted, "We don't like him......he thinks he's smart because momma married his daddy."

(194)

As they looked over their daughter's report card, Mrs. Pushover told her husband, "Poor Kelli is failing three courses. I'll bet she's taking it hard." Mr. Pushover growled, "That's why she fails. When she should be upstairs studying, she's out with some boy, taking it hard."

(195)

The farmer had caught a traveling salesman with his daughter, and was marching them towards the church. As they walked, the farmer remarked, "Ben Franklin once said, "They who can give up essential liberty to obtain a little temporary safety deserve neither liberty or safety." The salesman snarled, "What that supposed to mean?" The farmer answered gently, "I was in your predicament once, Sonny, and if I was you ….I'd tell me to shoot."

(196)

The preacher knocked at a lady's door one morning and announced, "I met your little son on his way to class. He told me you were sick, so I decided to pay a call. That afternoon when the boy came home from school, she asked him, "Why did you lie to the preacher?" he retorted hotly, "I didn't lie, I thought you WERE sick…last night I distinctly heard Daddy tell you to turn over and take your medicine."

(197)

A golfer stumbled into the country club bar, downed six straight Scotches, then told the bartender, "I've had crushing news. My wife ran off with my golf buddy." The barkeep consoled, "you'll soon replace her." The man sobbed, "Yes, but not him…. He's the only guy on the course I could beat !"

(198)

A man was driving along the highway when he saw a long-haired hippie on the shoulder of the road, frantically waving both arms in a signal for help. So he pulled over and asked what was wrong. The hippie screeched, "I've been raped !" Three big truck drivers picked me up and raped me !" The man said, "Get in my car and I'll take you to the hospital." The hippie boomed, "Hospital, hell ! Take me to the barber shop...I want to get my hair cut." Don't you wish every city had a billboard sponsored by the Barber's Union showing a picture of a hippie, with the words, "CLEAN UP AMERICA- GET A HAIRCUT ?"

(199)

Everyone in the Fudpucker family reunion was impressed by the delicious pie Granny Fudpucker served. Aunt Ophella gushed, "it's not only good, it's gorgeous ! How did you make this pretty scalloped crust ?" Granny blushed, It was easy....I used Grandpaw's false teeth."

(200)

Mike & Helen had been married for ten years when one evening at dinner Mike announced his intention of taking a mistress. His wife was shocked, but Mike pointed out that his two partners, Jim and Bob, both had mistresses and their wives had adjusted to the situation very nicely. "All three girls dance in the chorus of the same night club," Mike explained, "and tomorrow night, I'm going to take you to see them." The next evening, Mike and Helen went to the night club, and when the showgirls began their opening number, Mike said, "The blonde on the left is Jim's. The redhead next to her is Bob's. And the pretty brunette on the end is mine." Helen stared at the girls long and hard before answering: "You know something, darling ? Of the three, I like ours best."

(201)

The toddler had been pestering Daddy for a true bedtime story. Dad said, "Okay. One winter evening I looked out the window at the dark cloudy sky. I remarked, it looks like it's gonna be a long, hard one tonight. Your mother looked over at me and whispered, "I sure hope so !" and nine months later, YOU were born."

(202)

Seeing a new clerk at the hardware store, Peter Nundinger asked, "What happened to Sam, who used to work here ?" The new man explained, "Sam was caught in the act with his neighbor's wife and in the excitement he died of heart failure." Peter popped out, "I thought Sam's heart was in perfect condition !" The clerk replied, "It was … ….until his neighbor ran a knife through it."

(203)

Billy: "How'd you like me to slip you 12 inches tonight ?" Helen: "I don't think you could get it up 4 times in a row."

(204)

"Isn't the moon lovely ?" She sighed. "If you say so. " answered her date. "Personally, I'm in no position to say."

(205)

"My wife's an angel," observed the little man to the chap sitting next to him at the bar. "You're lucky," answered the other. "Mine's still alive."

(206)

Sue Ann the mountain girl, was sittin' on her front porch one day in a rather "exposed" position when Clem came by. "What's that ?" Said Clem. "That's my washing machine," said Sue. "Well." He suggested, "Then how about doing my laundry for me ?" So she took him inside and did his washing. A few days later Clem passed again and asked Sue to do his washing again. But she replied, "Man, with what little washing YOU'VE got, you can do it by hand !"

(207)

After going through the line at a crowded cafeteria, the three rambunctious teenage boys found they were forced to share a table with a kindly-looking old lady. One of the lads decided to have a bit of fun at the woman's expense and, nudging one of his buddies under the table, suddenly remarked, "Did your folks ever get married ?" "Nope." Replied his table-mate, picking up the put-on. "How about yours ?" "They never bothered," answered the first young man. "That's nothing," Interrupted the third, "My mother doesn't even know who my father is." The elderly woman looked up from her coffee and said sweetly, "Excuse me, but would one of you little bastards please pass the sugar ?"

(208)

During camouflage training in Louisiana, a private disguised as a tree trunk had made a sudden move that was spotted by a visiting general. "You Simpleton !" the officer barked. "Don't you know that jumping and yelling the way you did, you could have endangered the lives of the entire company ?" "Yes sir," the soldier answered apologetically. "But, if I may say so, I did stand still when a flock of pigeons used me for target practice. And I never moved a muscle when a large dog pee'd on my lower branches. But when two squirrels ran up my pants leg and I heard the bigger one say, "Let's eat one now and save the other until winter - that did it."

(209)

A young woman went into the drug store and asked for a quart of strychnine. The clerk asked her what she wanted it for, and she told him, "My boyfriend and I had a fight, and I'm going to kill myself." So he went into the back room and mixed up a quart of milk of magnesia. She paid him and started to leave, but just as she reached the door, she called out, "Well, so long....I'll see you in hell !" He replied, "Yea, you'll crap, too !"

(210)

He ran his hands over her shoulders. They were smooth, warm and promising. Slowly he began moving his fingers down, stopping once in a while to make closer inspection of choice spots. As he stroked her smooth belly, he could feel her quiver to his touch. His hand moved tenderly up to her back, and slid slowly down over her gorgeous back-end. Gently he moved over her legs, so smooth, so firm, not flabby. He stopped and said, "This gal can't loose, when she races at Gulf Stream next week !"

(211)

He picked up a nice looking broad in a bar, spent fifteen or twenty bucks on drinks, and suggested they wind their way to his pad and listen to the hi-fi. On the way she said, "I sure am hungry...couldn't we stop for a snack ?" So he took in a restaurant where she ordered pate de fole gras, two shrimp cocktails, a sirloin strip, broiled lamb chops with the bone in, a whole roasted chicken, and a few other things. She ate it all like there was no tomorrow, and washed it down with a couple of Liqueurs and coffee. Then he said. "Do you always eat like THIS ?" And she smiled and replied, "No, only when I'm having my PERIOD !"

(212)

Two fellows died and went to heaven. St. Peter asked the first, "Did you ever commit adultery ?" "NEVER !" said the man. So he gave the fellow a Cadillac to ride in. Then St. Peter asked the second fellow who said, "Only once in a while." So St. Peter gave him a new Ford to ride in. In a minute one fellow started laughing and the other fellow asked him why, and the first fellow said. "Look ! There's our preacher on ROLLER SKATES !"

(213)

Do you know what hell is ? It's a beautiful nude blond sitting on a guy's lap. There is a keg of beer beside him. The keg of beer has a hole in the bottom of it and the blond hasn't.

(214)

The handsome President requested that the company psychiatrist further screen the three good-looking girls for the job of private secretary. Deciding to use a standard psychological ploy, the gentleman asked each of the applicants the same question - "How much do two and two make ?" The first young thing, a lovely blonde, whispered, "Four"; the second, a smashing brunette, responded with "Twenty-two"; while the third, a shapely redhead, answered, four or twenty-two." The following day, the consultant stopped by the Presidents office and gave his findings. "The first is solid and reliable, He opined. "The second has a vivid imagination but can't deal with reality. And the third is both clever and mature - she being the one I'd suggest we hire. What's your decision ?" "Well," the boss replied, after a moment of deep deliberation, "I think I want the one with the nice ass and big boobs !"

(215)

The old couple, celebrating their 50th wedding anniversary , went to the same hotel and the same room. "Paw," said the old lady, "Remember how anxious you were on our wedding night ?" Paw smiled and said, "I sure do, Maw…I was so anxious you didn't have time to take your stockings off. But tonight you've got time to knit yourself a pair !"

(216)

When a man came home and presented his wife with a bouquet of flowers, and it wasn't her birthday or anniversary or anything, she immediately became suspicious. So she said, "Now I suppose you expect me to lay spread eagle on the floor for a week !" He asked, "What's the matter, don't we have any vases ?"

(217)

A fellow woke up with a black eye. He asked his wife what happened. She said, "While you were sleeping you felt my arms and said, "What a smooth finish." Then you reached further and said, "What perfect headlights." Then you reached even further and said, "Who in the hell left the garage door open ?" That's when I let you have it with my elbow !"

(218)

A fellow was in a bar drinking Manhattans. He said to the bartender, "Give me another Manhattan, but leave out the fruit this time." And the lacy lad with the lavender, looked down the bar, spoke up and said "Up yours you mother ! I didn't ask for the first one !"

(219)

Two old friends, both prosperous businessmen, hadn't seen each other in some time and happened to meet on the beach at Miami. "What brings you here, Jack ?" Asked one. "Actually Fred, a tragedy. My business was burned to the ground, and I'm taking a vacation on part of the $250,000 insurance money." "What a coincidence," responded Fred. "My business was destroyed by a flood and I got almost a million in insurance." After a moment of thoughtful silence, Jack leaned close to his friend and whispered: "Tell me, Fred - how do you start a flood ?"

(220)

Two wives talking. "I always tell my husband how much I love him," said the first, "Well, DO YOU ?" asked the second. "Hell no," replied the first, "But it makes him get through a lot quicker !"

(221)

A 70 year old man met a fellow geriatric on the street one day and asked him what he'd been doing lately. The friend said he'd just spent six months in jail, after being convicted of rape, "Rape !" Shouted the first man. "At your age ? That's the most ridiculous thing I ever heard of." " I know," replied the other, "but I was so flattered, I pled guilty."

(222)

A hillbilly just down from the mountains stuck this head out of a telephone booth and hollered at a passing stranger, "Hey mister....how do you flush this thing ?"

(223)

Old man Dew's oldest kid, who was named Mountain Dew in honor of his pop's vocation , started to school. The teacher said, "What's your name, little boy ?" Mount said, "You'll laugh, but I'll give you a hint, teacher….it'll tickle your innards !" So the teacher said, "OK, Dick, you sit down now."

(224)

These airline stewardesses can handle any situation. A beauteous fly girl had two men on the same plane, to New York, both giving her a fit to try to make a date with her, begging for her address, phone number and everything. One even went as far as to pull his New York apartment key out of his pocket, whisper his address and apartment number to her, and begged her to, "Come see me tonight after we land" She smiled, took the key, walked to the plane's front seat where her OTHER admirer was breathing heavily, handed him the key, gave him the address and apartment number and said, "Come up tonight at nine"

(225)

Stopping to pay a call on some of his suburban constituents, the congressman found that they were having a party and volunteered to return at a more convenient time. "Don't go," the host begged "Were playing a game that you might enjoy. We blind fold the women and then they try to guess the identity of the men by feeling their genitals." "How dare you suggest such a thing to a man of my dignity and stature ?" The politician roared. "You might as well play," The host urged. "Your name's already been guessed three times."

(226)

The kid ran out of the topless bar. The doorman grabbed him and asked him what was the matter. The kid said, "My mama told me if I ever looked at anything bad I'd turn to stone........and I can feel it starting !"

(227)

When a funeral procession passed a golf course where four men were preparing to tee off for their regular Saturday-afternoon game, one of them turned toward the street, removed his cap and held it over his heart. "Why did you do that ?" asked his partner. "Well," replied the fellow, "I thought it was the least I could do for my wife."

(228)

After an examination, the curvaceous blond phoned her gynecologist and asked, "Doctor, would you see if by chance I left my panties in your office ?" He looked in the examining room returned to the phone and told her, "I'm afraid they're not here." "Sorry to trouble you, doctor," she replied. "I'll try the dentist."

(229)

The sexy coed was being driven back to college by her wealthy father's chauffeur when a tire blew out. Seeing that the chauffeur couldn't remove the hubcap, the girl reached for the toolbox and asked, "Do you want a screwdriver ?" "Might as well," he muttered. "I sure can't get this damn hubcap off."

(230)

A lady got on a plane with her new baby and happened to sit down by a drunk. After they took off, the drunk roused up, took a hard look at the kid and said, "Lady, I've never seem a more REPULSIVE brat in my life...I just SHUDDER when I look at him !" The lady called the stewardess and said, "Get him away from me, or I'll sue this airline for a million dollars !" So the hostess took the drunk to the back, returned and said, "Now don't be upset, madam. Just relax while I get you a cup of coffee and dig up a banana for your monkey !"

(231)

Helen Patricia was complaining to Aunt Bonnie, "That husband of mine never takes me anywhere. All he thinks about is crops and cattle." Bonnie replied , "You poor thing. Charley thinks about me all the time. He even puts me before his prize bull." Helen Patricia, "Oh, my husband does that, too. But I always jump out of the way !"

(232)

It is tacitly understood that he would give her a gorgeous diamond dinner ring for Christmas, and she would give him a solid gold Rolex watch...yet under the tree the young couple found packages, which, when opened, disclosed a house dress for her and a pair of britches for him. Both angry, he threw his new pants up on the chandelier and she threw her new dress on the floor and stepped on it. But when they went to breakfast, there by the plate of each, they found exactly the presents they wanted. The couple smiled shamefacedly, and after breakfast she picked up her dress, he took down his pants, and they had a Merry Christmas !

(233)

The kid was going home from the grocery. He had one hand in his pocket and was carrying his mama a loaf of bread in the other. He met his preacher coming down the street, In religious tones, to impress the lad, the preacher said, "You have the staff of life in one hand...what do you have in the other ?" The kid answered, "A loaf of bread."

(234)

The bellhop took the crippled couple to their room, then stayed and peeped through the keyhole. He saw the girl screw one leg off. He saw the man screw one leg off....then they did just what he expected, started screwing their heads off.....

(235)

A Marine was taking a newly acquired girlfriend for a ride in the country when they came upon a bull and a cow increasing the bovine population. "What are they doing ?" asked the girl. "He is scaring her," said the Marine. "Why don't you scare me ?" Requested the girl.... and being a Marine, he had the situation well in hand. They drove a few miles farther and she said, "Scare me again," and the Marine complied. Then a few miles further and , "Scare me again." She cried, and the Marine said, "BOO, you little sex manic !"

(236)

The recent bride was seriously considering having a baby, but was deathly afraid, due to all the tales she had heard about childbirth. So she asked her mother to describe the pains to her. "Take hold of your lower lip, dear and pinch it as tight as you possibly can ." The daughter did, and said, "I believe I can stand that." The mother added, "Now then, grasping it firmly between thumb and forefinger, stretch your lower lip, over your skull, and staple it to the back of your neck !" The bride said, "You can bet your back-end there are not going to be any kids in this family !"

(237)

A carpenter was doing work for Johnny's folks. Every time the carpenter got out another tool to work with, little Johnny would say, "My pop's got TWO of those." The carpenter finally had to use the bathroom, and Johnny followed him in there. "I'll bet your pop hasn't got two of THESE," said the carpenter. And Johnny replied, "No, but he's got ONE that will make TWO of yours !"

(238)

Then there was this pretty young thing who ran into the police station and reported, "I have just been raped by a stupid imbecile." "How do you know he was a stupid imbecile." Asked the desk sergeant. "He must have been," she said "I had to show him what to do !"

(239)

They were making passionate love in her bedroom when the telephone began to ring. She pulled away and got up to answer the phone. In a few seconds she returned to bed and her boyfriend asked, "Who was that on the phone ?" My husband, she replied, as she snuggled up even closed to her bed partner, "He wanted to tell me that he'll be late coming home because he is playing poker with you and some of the other fellows !"

(240)

Billy Peters, the star halfback for the championship State Collage Football Team, broke his leg in scrimmage two days before the big game of the year. On Friday, the local paper printed the headline, TEAM WILL PLAY WITHOUT PETERS ! After the Dean of the school raised hell with the paper, they made sure it was changed in the Saturday edition. On Saturday morning, the headline read, TEAM WILL PLAY WITH PETERS OUT.

(241)

Then there was this 90 year old man who was telling his friends about a new pill he had heard about that would guarantee he could satisfy a 20 year old girl. "It does have it's drawbacks, the first time I took them I got one hell of a stiff neck because I didn't swallow them fast enough !"

(242)

The horny gynecologist starts stroking the patient's breasts. "Do you know what I'm doing ?" he asked quietly. "yes," she replies, "You're inspecting for abnormal skin condition or discharge preparatory to an internal examination." The doctor drops his pants, leaps onto the table and starts pumping. "Now do you know what I'm doing ?" he gasps "Yes," the woman replies. "You're getting herpes."

(243)

Jim and George went duck hunting. They got in a row boat and went out to the middle of the lake when George's shot gun discharged accidentally and blew a hole in the bottom of the boat. Jim said, "Stick your finger in the hole or the boat will sink and we'll go down with it !" George sadly replied, "No use, the hole is too big !" Jim replied, "I know what you mean.... I'm having the same trouble at home...."

(244)

Doctor to a pregnant woman : "Mrs. Phelps, why did you wait until you were forty years old to have a baby ?" Mrs. Phelps replied, "Well, the first husband I had was a preacher and he wanted to save everything. My second husband was a policeman and all he wanted to do was protect it. But now I am married to a farmer....and he plowed right in !"

(245)

A couple were in a restaurant deciding what to order. They finally asked for steak. The waiter told them they were all out of steak. So the couple then asked for pork or lamb chops. The waiter told them he was awfully sorry, but they were out of those, too So the woman asked, "Well, do you have any meat at all ?" The waited replied, "Yes, ma'am, we have delicious beef tongue ?" The woman said, "Oh, dear, I wouldn't eat anything from an animal's mouth !" The waiter said, "Well, lady, you could have some eggs."

(246)

When asked how he'd like to leave this world, the senior citizen replied, "Same as I came in.......naked and next to a nice lady."

(247)

The bartender presented the conventioneer with the bill, and the customer was outraged. "New York in the most expensive place in the world," he complained. "Why, back in Sioux City, you can drink as much as you want without paying, sleep in a fancy hotel for free and wake up and find fifty dollars on the pillow." "Come on, now" questioned the bartender. "has that ever happened to you ?" "No," the man admitted. "But it happens to my wife all the time."

(248)

"I suppose," snarled the leathery sergeant to the private, "That when you're discharged from the Army, you'll wait for me to die, just so you can spit on my grave." "Not me," observed the private. "When I get out of the Army, I never want to stand in line again."

(249)

Two drunks standing at the bar when one said. "The last time I was here I fell and broke a couple ribs. I went to the doctor and after taping my broken ribs, the doctor said to me, "Remember, no relations for three weeks," I told him, "That's fine, Doc. Without them coming over all the time, the wife and I catch up with our screwing !"

(250)

A drunk got onto a Pullman, and accidentally crawled into the wrong berth, with a lady who had a wooden leg. There was some jostling and shoving, and pretty soon the wooden leg was sticking through the curtains. The porter came by and said, "Hey, what you got in there, a wheelbarrow ?" The drunk answered, "Yes, and don't turn it over, because I'm in it."

(251)

When little Johnny came in the house covered with mud, his mother really hit the ceiling. "Johnny she cried, "What in the heck were you doing to get so dirty ?" Johnny replied, "We were playing farm. I was the pig and had to crawl around in the mud." His mother said, "Did you have to pick the dirtiest job in the lot ?" He said, "Oh, I didn't....little Dottie was a chicken, and you should see the mess she made when she tried to lay an egg !"

(252)

The widow had her husbands body cremated, took the ashes home, poured them out on the table, and said, "Sam, I always wanted a fur coat, and you never got me one. I'm buying one with your life insurance money. I always wanted a diamond bracelet and you never got me one. I'm buying one with the money in your savings account. You always wanted a blow job and I never gave you one. Here is one now. POOF...POOF...POOF...!

(253)

A man went to the Doctor and was told that he was in the advanced stages of a 24-hour virus and would be dead before morning. He went home and told his wife, "This is my last chance for sex, so I'm gonna get all I can." They did it at 8, 9, 10, 11 and again at midnight. At one o'clock, he reached for her again. She said, "No ! Enough is enough !" "After all, you don't have to get up tomorrow."

(254)

Homer and Helen were working on their yard when a neighbor woman drove past and honked. Helen waved, but Homer just shrugged. Helen asked, "Didn't you recognize her ?" Homer sneered, "Yes, but I can't stand that slut. She's always bragging that her husband is a better lay than I am." Helen hollered, "why that lying bitch....he is not !"

(255)

One morning Mrs. Smith had to go to the chiropractor, and she took her 5-year old son along. When they returned, the little boy went to the barn to see his daddy. All of a sudden, the boy said, "Oh, look, daddy, that rooster is giving that hen a back treatment !" Farmer Smith laughed and asked, "Now where did you learn to call it that ?" The little boy replied, "That's what the doctor called it when he did it to mommy."

(256)

A traveling salesman's car broke down way out in the country one rainy night, and he trudged soggily up to the nearest farm house. His knock was answered by a bearded old farmer, who insisted he come in at once and dry off. Once inside, he met a beautiful bosomy wench of about nineteen years, dressed only in a ragged slip. "Say !" he exclaimed, "Ill bet you're the farmer's daughter." The girl laughed, "Not on your life, chum ! I'm a sales person too, I've been here 3 days, this farmer is really something !"

(257)

A car was parked on a dark, lonely, country road. A passing motorist stopped and called out, "What seems to be the trouble ?" Tire down ?" From the back seat, a man's voice answered, "Nope....didn't have to . She was ready !"

In order to save money for a new color television, a woman was serving lots of economy dishes like ham and potatoes. One night her husband said to her, "I'm getting sick and tired of ham and potatoes. If I come home tomorrow night and find a dish of ham and potatoes on the table , I'll stick it up your rear !" But the next night when he came home, she fixed ham and potatoes again, so he started chasing her, and they wound up in the bedroom with the door locked. Their two kids, who had been watching the activities , ran to peek through the key hole. The little boy got there first, and the little girl asked him, "Does he have it all in ?" The little boy said, "All except two of the potatoes,"

As a fellow pulled into the town's leading hamburger stand in his brand new car, a joker leaned over and asked, "Anybody get cut in that wreck ?" The car owner replied calmly, "No, but your wife got banged a little."

Bill was trying to sell Jim on the advantages of married life. "You're no good as a bachelor," he said. "Now, if you were married to my wife, you wouldn't be committing adultery three times a week." Jim said, "Oh God, she promised me she wouldn't tell you !"

A disc Jockey ends his show with..... "This program has been brought to you by the Mike Sass Used Car Lot. So don't forget folks, for the best deal in town, just look up Mike Sass..."

(262)

A fellow was puttering around his home workshop in unusually good spirits, prompting his wife to ask, "Why are you so happy ?" He replied, "Because I'm planning to get a little tonight." She said, "Oh, really, where ?"

(263)

Paul Revere shook his sleeping wife in the middle of the night. She said, "What are you doing that for ?" He said, "I have to wake everybody up, I'm a Minute Man !" She replied, "No question about that !"

(264)

Back in the days when women wore dresses down to the floor, a preacher was making home visitations. One woman barely had time to bathe six of her seven children before he arrived, so she told the dirty one, "Billy Bob, you crawl under my skirt and stay there until the parson leaves. The preacher came in, patted all visible children's heads, called them by their names, asked about their school work, and then settled in to chat with the mother. After a while he glanced down near her feet and hollered, "Why, hello there, Bill, I didn't see you before !" Billy Bob replied, "You wouldn't see me NOW, if Momma hadn't tooted,"

(265)

A traveling salesman stopped at a New England farm house and asked to spend the night. The farmer told him they only had two beds, and he would have to check with his teenage daughter. Then he went to the daughter and said, "Could you possibly share your bed with a traveling salesman tonight. You may call for me if he tries anything." The girl replied, "Well, I'd rather not, but I suppose it will be all right." So the family retired, and a few hours later, the young girl began to yell, "FATHER ! FATHER ! The salesman retorted, "Just what do you think I've got.........a telephone pole ?"

(266)

A farmer was about to turn into his private road and found the way blocked by a parked car with a man and woman in it. The farmer waved his fist and shouted, "Get out of there, you bastard !" The man in the car looked up and said indignantly, "Sir ! I'll have you know, I'm Pastor Bill Button." The farmer retorted, "Mister, I don't care if you're in up to her nose. This is my lane, so PULL OUT !

(267)

Lizzy Jane's mother wouldn't let her go out with her boyfriend one Saturday night, so Lizzy got down on the floor and laid on top of a knot hole. Her boyfriend crawled under the house and took advantage of the situation. Pretty soon, the girl got to moaning and squirming, and her mother said, "Child, get up from the there, you're having a fit." But Lizzy just stayed there groaning, so Mom walked over, pulled her up, and said, "Lord a mercy, child ! It's a snake ! stand over in the corner while I kick It's head off !"

(268)

The hiccuping customer approached the beautiful blonde airline clerk and asked for a ticket he'd reserved. "Here you are," she said. Then, after he'd paid once, she added, "And now you owe us ANOTHER two hundred dollars !" He howled, "What ?" She smiled sweetly and said, "I was just kidding. But it cured your hiccups, didn't it ? He replied. "It sure did, honey. Now, how would you like to clean up this mess that's running down my legs ?"

(269)

Grandpa Whitebeard was in the village store when a younger soldier came in and ordered a dozen bags of saltpeter for the camp. After he left, grandpa asked the clerk, "What was that he ordered ?" The clerk said, "Saltpeter. The boys at the camp use it in their food, so they won't have amorous desires." Gramp said "How about letting me have a dime's worth ?" The astonished clerk said, "But Gramps, you're over ninety years old. You surely don't need saltpeter !" Grandpa replied, "Well, I though maybe if I sniffed a pinch up my nose, I could get it off my mind."

(270)

The bellboy opened the door of the hotel room and saw a man sitting on the side of the bed playing with himself. "Did you order a bottle, sir ?" he asked. The man said, "Hell, no. I'm so drunk now I don't know the name of the woman I'm humping."

(271)

Three convicted felons were lined up to die by firing squad. When the first man's turn came , he shouted, "TORNADO !" The squad ran for cover, and he escaped. The second man didn't think it would work twice , but figured he had nothing to lose. When the guns were pointed at him, he Yelled, "KILLER BEES !" Again the squad ran for cover, and he too, got away. The third man was amazed by the easiness of it all. When his turn came, he stepped up confidently and hollered, "FIRE !"

(272)

A wealthy customer walked into the Peacock Lounge. Hanging onto his arm was a sexy chick in a brand new full length fur coat. When the sexpot had gone to the real pot, the bartender told the man, "The other night I heard you promise that doll a new car if she'd shack-up with you. How come you bought her the mink instead ?" The guy winked, "They don't make imitation cars."

(273)

Homer Fudpucker shuffled into the house and told his wife, "I saw the doctor about the rash I've been getting on my tallywhacker and ....well, er... he told me I can't make love." She smiled, "My goodness, dear, you didn't need to go to the doctor.....I could've told you that."

(274)

Then there was the man who walked into the Hospital Emergency Room looking like he had just been run over by a truck ! The admission clerk asked "What in the world happened to you ?" The man replied, "Well, I came home from work with lip stick on my shorts. My wife threw them out the window and I was still in them !"

(275)

The professor included the following question in his Psychology Exam ! "Why do some humans insist on illicit sex rather than true married love ?" One of the football players in the back of the room yelled, "NO MOTHER IN LAW !"

(276)

We as husbands, are forgetting how we slave to please our wife, in trade, for constant petting, takes our money the rest of our life !"

(277)

Did you ever stop to think....there are three things that are not worth anything until they get hard. Ice and cement are the first two !

(278)

The new teacher was asking each little pupil to get up and give her their name. One little boy got up and said, "Peter Period." So she asked, unbelieving, several more times, and got the same answer. At lunch time the new teacher went in and asked the principal. "Do we have a Peter Period in this school ?" and the principal said, "Hell, no...we don't even have time for a coffee break !"

(279)

My wife wrote this before we were married ! I've made love in a Chrysler, A Lincoln and a Rolls. I've got hot in a Chevy, A Buick and an Olds. I've done it in a Plymouth, A Dodge and Pontiac. I've been thrilled in a Mercury, A Ford and Cadillac. I've bedded down in many cars, for loving, not for sleep. But then a tragedy occurred....I got knocked up in a Jeep !

(280)

Every night George came home ready for sex but Sally always had an excuse. So finally George really got fed up, and he brought Sally home a package, inside of which were six little black kittens. Sally said, "What are these for ?" He replied, "They're pall bearers. Yours is evidently dead, and should be buried."

(281)

A teeny-bopper came home from school and shyly told her Mom, "The school nurse says you might have to take me to the doctor for a Rabbit Test." Mother was still in the bedroom sobbing two hours later when the living room phone rang. She heard an excited whoop, then the little girl appeared in the doorway and said, "It's all right, Mom. You don't have to take me after all. They found the dog that bit me."

(282)

A young college student's wife was expecting any day, but he had to leave and go back to school. In order that friends at school wouldn't know of his marriage, or his wife's pregnancy, they had arranged that she would wire him, "pillow has arrived." Three weeks after he got back to school he received the telegram. It said, "Three pillows arrived.....two with tassels."

(283)

One of the gentlemen farmers was having a big masquerade party, so one neighbor couple dressed as a cow and a bull to go to the party. Being late, they decided to just walk the short distance across a field, rather than driving way around in the car. In the middle of the pasture they were suddenly discovered by a real bull which charged them full speed ahead. "Oh my God, what are we going to do ?" shrieked the wife in her cow costume. Her husband, the bull, calmly replied, "I'm just going to stand here and eat grass, but why don't you just tell him you have a headache !"

(284)

"Tell me about your daylight fantasies," said the psychiatrist to the young matron. "Do you consider doing housework in the nude ?" Do you wonder how the brush of a feather duster feels against your naked nipples ? Have you thought of relieving your lustful instincts with the end of a broom handle ? The patient blushed, "Why, doctor, you should be ashamed of your self." You're nothing but a peeping tom !"

(285)

A hillbilly matron saw a store display of seductive nightgowns. "What're those ?" she asked. The clerk explained, "They're sexy lingerie. You wear them to bed to get some action started. Would you like to buy one ?" The country women sighed, "Twouldn't do no good. When Paw and me hit the sheets every night, we're both too tired to do anything but screw and sleep."

(286)

A mother took her young son to the pediatrician because his boy part wasn't growing like it should. The doctor suggested, "Give him a slice of burnt toast every day." Next morning there was a whole loaf of burnt toast on the breakfast table. The boy looked at it and wailed, "I can't swallow all of that !" His Mom said, "Just take one piece, son. The rest is for your father."

(287)

Girls. Do you gripe about your husband snoring ? Why ? Actually, it assures you he's home nights ! Besides, a man's snoring is the sweetest music in the world...if you don't believe it, ask a widow friend !

(288)

The newly wedded kids were spending their first night in her parent's home, The groom, a deeply religious lad, insisted when they were ready for bed that first they kneel and pray. This touched the bride, who next morning dashed down the stairs, telling her folks, "Last night Jimmy and I did something we've never done before, and we plan to do it every night from now on !" Her old man said, "Yeah, that's what your mother and I thought , too !"

(289)

Sam kept telling his friend Joe about the wonderful police dog he had. Finally Joe went over to see Sam's police dog, but instead of a police dog, there was a big mongrel up on the back of another dog, humping away. Joe sneered, "Man, that doesn't look like no police dog to me !" Sam replied, "Shhhh-hh, he's in the secret service and he's disguised....right now he's pumping her for information !"

(290)

Somebody advertised a Chihuahua to give away and the paper printed Uncle Hardy's address by mistake. A lady came to his door and asked, "Is your wife home ?" He answered no. She said, "Do you have a Chihuahua to give me ?" Hardy grinned, "if Chihuahua means 12 inches in Spanish, I sure got one for you !"

(291)

CLASSIC ! A secretary got a job at Zenith. After working there a while she noticed that all the other secretaries had their names on the doors under those of the executives. So she asked her boss about this. He didn't say a word.....just took her in his office, locked the door, undressed her, laid her out on the couch, then undressed himself, pointed to his little pointer and said, "This is Quality....remember our slogan here at Zenith.... The Quality Goes In Before The Name Goes On !"

(292)

Bill Hunt came into the office nursing a black eye and grumbling, "It was so dark last night, I couldn't see two feet in front of me." Sam Flocked asked, "Did you walk into a door ?" Bill moaned, "No, the two feet I couldn't see were those of her husband !"

(293)

The new bride went into the drug store and asked for a bottle of men's deodorant, so the clerk said, "The ball type ?" and she said, "no, for under his arms."

(294)

Homer came home late one night, tiptoed to the bedroom, and found his side of the bed already occupied. Homer shook his wife awake and demanded, "What is he doing in my place ?" She asked, "Do you really mind dear ?" Homer hollered, "Of course, I mind ! You could roll over in your sleep and hurt him." She yawned, "I guess you're right....be a love, and put the baby back in his crib."

(295)

Little Mary went next door to play with little Willie. Willie's mother told her, "He's been a bad boy and has to sit in the corner. He can't play with you today." Mary sighed, "Then I guess I'll have to play with myself." Willie shouted, "Don't do that...that's what I'm sitting in the corner for !"

(296)

A farmer was injured in a threshing accident and needed immediate transfusions. The nearest blood bank was too far away, so the doctor took samples from everyone on the farm for testing. When he came out of the lab, the patient's wife asked, "Is it good or bad ?" The doctor replied, "A little of both. You and your husband have the same blood type, but the children and the hired man are all type O."

(297)

A women went to the clinic for artificial insemination. To her amazement, the staff physician was wearing no pants. "Doctor !" she shrieked, "What is the meaning of this outrage ?" He answered curtly, "I'm sorry, madam, but we're out of the bottle stuff. You'll have to settle for draft today."

(298)

I promised my wife I'd give up drinking. Which proves one thing: People will say anything when they're drunk ! Those first few months after taking the pledge are the hardest. You feel so silly drinking Pepsi Cola out of a brown paper bag.

(299)

I tried hypnotism to quit cigarettes, but something must have gone wrong. I still smoke, but every time I do, I get verrry sleepy

(300)

I just saw a wild bumper sticker. It said: HONK IF YOU LOVE QUITE !

(301)

I'm not going to say he cheats at golf. Let's just put it this way : Last year he wore out three clubs and six erasers.

(302)

You have to be a little suspicious of anyone who writes down their score and then wipes his fingerprints off the pencil.

(303)

A lonely widow, who hadn't been laid since her husband passed on five years ago, hired a strapping young lad as a farm hand. One day she was watching through the window as he worked in the garden. The sun was very hot and he removed his shirt and shoes. Finally he stripped to his undershorts. This inspired her to tear off all her own clothes and jump on the bed, where she lay with her legs spread out, screaming, "HOMER, HOMER COME IN HERE !" When the young man arrived, she pointed at her fur patch and smiled, " Did you ever see anything like this before ?" He gulped, "Gosh, no ma'am.....you hold steady, and I'll get the mop handle and kill it !"

(304)

An 80-year-old man visits a whore and says he wants it three times. "Let me nap for twenty minutes between screws and you hold my dork with both hands while I sleep," he tells the skeptical hooker. Sure enough, they screw, she grabs his dick with both hands, he sleeps for twenty minutes, they screw again, she grabs, he sleeps and he gets it up a third time. "I understand the nap," says the girl, "But tell me, what does it do for you when I hold your dork with both hands ?" "Nothing," says the old man. "But last time I screwed a whore, she stole my wallet."

(305)

Junior came running into the house, shouting, "Momma ! Momma ! I saw Sis and the hired man out behind the barn ! He pulled a big snake out of his overalls, pushed Sis down, and poked that snake between her legs to scare her !" His mother, whose mind was on the eggs she was candling, asked without listening. "Was your sister hurt ?" Junior exclaimed, "No, she just laughed....but when she pulled out the snake, you could sure tell it was dead."

(306)

The patient was a bit shy about baring her breast until Doctor Wellby assured her, "You just couldn't have anything funnier than some I've seen." So she gingerly unhooked her bra. Her left boob popped up like a parasol, while its mate sagged halfway to the floor. The kindly old physician guffawed, "I was wrong....I never saw anything to equal those ! How'd it happen ?" She stammered, blushing, "My husband sucks the right breast in his sleep all night." The doctor replied, "I do the same thing, but my nurse doesn't share your problem." The woman said, "Yes, I know....but my husband falls out of bed a lot."

(307)

Two drunks, both smashed, were sitting at the bar. One said, "I've got to tinkle," and trotted off to the pot. When he came back, the other lush requested, "Before you sit down, go drain a few drops for me." The first drunk obligingly returned to the restroom, grunted and groaned, and wound up messing in his pants. Staggering back to the bar, he stuck out a fist and POW ! He flattened the other drunk. From the floor, his friend groaned, "Why did you do that ?" The standing drunk screamed, "You KNOW why, you thoughtless jerk ! Why didn't you tell me you had to do number two !"

(308)

A tiny girl told her mother, "I'm not ever going to speak to big sister again !" Mom asked gently, "Are you jealous because she brought home that pretty fur coat ?" The toddler pouted, "No, I hate her because she's mean. It was cruel to bait that trap with a helpless kitten." The mother exploded, "I don't know what you are talking about !" The little girl huffed, "Well, I do. I heard her tell her friends, "look at this beautiful mink I got WITH JUST A LITTLE PUSSY !"

(309)

A traveling salesman wrote to the home office, "A funny thing happened when I got to Omaha. I was flirting with this pretty little waitress at the diner, and she seemed to be enjoying it. After a while, I whispered to the fellow beside me, "I think I could get some of that if I tried." He answered , "I think not. She's my wife." The doctor says I will be out of the cast and back on the road by Thursday."

(310)

So you are over 50 ! Yesterday, when I was young... The whole world knew how I was hung...But now I'm old and getting gray....It's harder getting gals to play...They look at me and look away...but those who take a chance all say..."He's still as fresh as yesterday."

(311)

One man in the New Fathers' Waiting Room kept holding his crotch. Another fellow stopped pacing long enough to wonder, "Are you hurting to get your wife home to bed again ?" He answered dreamily, "no, I was just meditating on how easy this is for us men, the little part we have in the thing. Slip her the lucky wand, and ZAP....you're in business. You lose a little here, and you gain a little heir."

(312)

"Just relax, young lady," said the kindly old DR. Fudpucker to the patient sprawled out on his examining table, "I've probed hundreds of ladies" hoochy-diddles before, and there's absolutely nothing for you to worry about." The young lady rasped, "Well, maybe not, but please be gentle...It's the first time I've had a doctor look in my sore throat from that end."

(313)

Mike went across the street to see Jock's new rifle with the telescoping sight. "You can really see a lot with this lens," He said zeroing in on Mike's house. "there goes the mailman to your front door. Your wife is letting him in. They went upstairs. I can see them in the bedroom. They took off their clothes." Mike thundered, "Give me that rifle ! I want to blew her brains out and shoot his cock off !" Jock handed him the gun and said, "Hurry up ....you can do both with one shot !"

(314)

Pastor Ashes got tired of having his evening catechism students straggle in halfway through the session. So he wrote on the blackboard, "THE PASTOR WILL MEET HIS CLASSES PROMPTLY AT 8 O'CLOCK." While he was out of the room, a smart aleck went up and erased the "C" from the word "CLASSES." At this, the whole group proceeded to roll on the floor in unholy glee. Pastor Ashes returned and saw at once what had cracked them up. Without a word, he walked to the board and erased the "L."

(315)

Did you hear about the young man - named Fido ? When we asked about the nickname, he replied, "It's my real handle. Mom named me because of something Dad said the first time they met." We asked, "Did he call her a dog ?" He answered , "No, he told her, "quit bitching....nothing will happen if we do it dog fashion !"

(316)

O.K., here's a question for you.....What begins with a "P" and ends with a "Y" and all men are crazy about it ? Sure you know....It's PAYDAY !

(317)

A night worker swore to let his beard grow until his favorite ball team won the pennant. His wife though this a hairy thing to do, and made no bones with him because of it. On the night our hero's heroes clinched the top slot, he took off early, stopped at a round the clock barber shop for a shave, then went home and slipped into bed. In total darkness, he grabbed his wife's fingers and ran them over his newly smooth chin. She moved closer to him and whispered, "Better make it quick, kid. Old whiskers will be home any minute."

(318)

On the night of her husband's birthday, Frigid Freda rolled over close to whisper, "What would you think if I gave you some real good loving ?"   Only half awake, he mumbled, "I would probably think I got into the wrong bed by mistake !"

(319)

A proud father told his teenage LASS, "Your boyfriend asked me for your hand today, and I consented." She protested, "But, Daddy, I don't want to leave Mother." He reassured her, "That's quite all right, I won't stand in the way of your happiness...I would sure appreciate it if you would take your mother with you."

(320)

An incredibly beautiful nurse was auctioning kisses at the charity bazaar. Mr. Fuddducker promised, I'll bid $500 if you promise to sneak into my bed next time I'm a patient at your place." She shouted, "You're on !" and sold him a smooch. As he left, the old lecher leered, "See you when I'm sick." She giggled, "Don't count on it, sucker...I work at the Maternity Hospital."

(321)

The young mother was visiting with her neighbor. My 2 year old son gave me quite a surprise the other day, when he put both hands on my breasts, rubbed them around, and said, "Ou,Ou" I guess he'd seen his Daddy playing and decided to try it. My husband and I had a good laugh at the baby's trick...but you should've seen his grandmother's face later, when he did the same thing to her !"

(322)

Helen and Patty went shopping for a bikini during their lunch break. When they got back to the office, one of their co-workers asked, "Well, did you buy anything ?" Both girls spoke up in unison and replied, "Hell no !" The damn price tags were bigger than the bottom half."

(323)

If you and your husband ever travel in Michigan, make sure right before you enter the little town of HELL, reach over and stroke "his" a couple of times. When you get back home, your husband is really going to enjoy telling the guys, "My wife and I went to Hell and I had a real hard on!"

(324)

The little boy asked Mommy, "Are you going to take the kitty with us when we visit Grandma ?" Mamma replied, "Why, of course not honey, what gave you the idea we were ?" The little boy explained, "Well, I heard Daddy tell the neighbor lady that her little mouse would have a great time when the "Old cat" went to Grandmas !"

(325)

The wife was bitching at her husband, "You S.O.B. you've never been on time in your entire life, not even for our wedding !" The husband replied, "That's BS, you should talk ! If you hadn't been LATE, there wouldn't even been a wedding !"

(326)

You know something ? people who don't believe in God are called, "Atheists." Those who don't believe in BIRTH CONTROL PILLS are called "Mommy" and "Daddy".

(327)

Helen Patricia and Ginny were talking one day and Helen Patricia said, "Ginny, you sure look bad this morning. You know, you really should sleep in your own bed once in a while !" Ginny yawned and replied, "I would really like to but that damn husband of yours keeps insisting on a motel !"

(328)

He asked the sweet little thing, Is it in ?" She answered, "Yes I believe so !" Then he asked, "Does it hurt ?" and she said, "No. In fact it really feels nice, and if the other shoe fits as well, I will buy the pair !"

(329)

The cute little gal went to her obstetrician who informed her that, yes, she was going to have a baby ! "You're full of it !", she acknowledged and then went on to call the poor Doctor every nasty name in the book. The Doctor stopped her and replied, "I don't understand why you are so shook up, I can see no problem from your pregnancy." She shook her head and said, "I sure as hell do...my husband is sterile !"

(330)

At your next party, want to have some fun ? Ask for a moments silence and say, "There's a queer in this room who thinks he is an owl !" You can bet, within seconds, someone will holler, "WHO !"

(331)

Have you ever heard about the brave husband who wrote a letter to his wife ? At the end of the letter, he wrote, "Well, I must close now but always remember, thinking about you makes me feel sexy all over, and the nearest cat house is over 30 minutes away !

(332)

You have heard that everything is BIG in Texas ! Well, that's not always true. A good Texas friend of ours and his wife had a eleven inch baby boy and you know it took him seventeen years to get twelve inches.

(333)

As a freshman in High School, my brother and I were talking about what we wanted to do in our adult life. After a 15 minute discussion, we came up with professions that would guarantee we would be millionaires. My brother decided he wanted to be an OBSTETRICIAN and I would be a MORTICIAN. That way, we would have them COMING AND GOING !

(334)

If you're a married man, here is a solution to your mother-in-law problems ! All you have to do is let your Father-in-law catch you in bed with the old bat. You can bet they won't be knocking at your door for a good long tome !

(335)

While visiting over the back fence, one woman remarked to the other, "You know, getting old is really hell. My old man's gotten so stubborn, he won't do it any way but "Dog Fashion. " The other woman replied, "You call THAT trouble ? My old man can only manage to do it coyote style....That's lay beside the hole and howl all night !

(336)

A worried voice on the doctor's telephone, "A mouse ran up my wife's honeypot." The doctor replied, I'll be over in ten minutes. In the meantime, try waving a piece of cheese between her legs." When the doctor arrived at the house, he was welcomed by the couple's young son, who showed him upstairs to a bedroom. There on the bed sat a frantic woman, leg spread wide, while her husband waved an open can of tuna over the opening. The doctor cried, "Idiot, I said to use cheese !" The man retorted, "I know that, you fool....but I've got to get the cat out first !"

(337)

THE SAD BRIDE TO BE: "There I was, waiting at the church....when I discovered he'd left me in the lurch...My , how that upset me ! But all at once he sent me a note...."I can't marry you today, he wrote, "MY WIFE WON'T LET ME!"

(338)

A magician walks into a Denver bar and announces, "I can give any man in this place a hard on in three seconds." A volunteer steps forward, the magician says "Abracadabra !" and the guy's rod stands at attention. "Now it'll go away as fast as it came if one person whistles." The bartender whistles and down it goes, instantly. Up steps an old codger, who hasn't had a hard on in 15 years. The magician did his stuff and the oldster pulled out a 45 "First guy who whistles, he says, "Gets it between the eyes."

(339)

HERE'S A TOAST YOU'VE GOT TO REMEMBER : Here's to the roses that are red and here's to the violets that are blue....I have a big one and I'm saving it just for you !

(340)

The first grade class was putting on a stage play for the PTA. One of the mother's leaned over to a gentleman sitting beside her and said, "LOOK AT LITTLE BILLY, HE IS ONLY 6 YEARS OLD AND HE ISN'T HALF AS BIG AS YOUR PETER !"

(341)

Why is it that women have such a time finding anything in their purse ? By the time they find a quarter for the pay toilet....it's too late to spend it !

(342)

Did you ever stop to think how much Sex is involved in our professions. For instance, brick masons lay bricks. Plumbers lay pipes, and tilers lay floors. But golfers, bowlers and tennis nuts just play around with their balls.

(343)

The company president walked into the office with a black eye. His Secretary asked, "Did you have a fight with your wife last night ? " He said, "I sure did, I was half asleep when she turned over, hugged me tight and told me she would like a little sex. Without thinking, I answered, "Honey, you're not getting any until you finish typing those letters I dictated!"

(344)

The teenage son pulled a prank on his Dad and the old man was not amused. The boy said, "What's the matter Pop, can't you take a joke?" Dad thought for a moment and replied, "Son, if I couldn't take a joke, I'd have left you in the hospital nursery!"

(345)

Did you ever stop and think how many of these Risqué stories wouldn't be funny if you didn't have a dirty mind?

(346)

You single girls are wasting money when you buy the new pregnancy tests! All you have to do is call your boy friends home. If his Mother answers and tells you he left town suddenly .... Well..... you know you're pregnant!

(347)

On the elevator, the office Romeo tried to make out with a shapely new secretary. He finally got up some nerve and asked her, "That wonderful perfume you have on, it smells so great, where did you buy it? I would sure like to get some for my secretary!" The little sexpot replied, "Mister, you wouldn't be doing your secretary any favor, when I wear it, all kinds of creeps and weirdoes try to talk to me!"

(348)

Here's a Wedding Announcement you won't want to use! "Ashes to ashes, dust to dust, we planned to stay single but the damn condom bust !"

(349)

Did you hear about the cute little sexpot who applied for a secretarial job? She could type 120 words per minute but she didn't get the job. It seems when she was filling out the application, she came to the question "SEX ?" She wrote down "Certainly Not!"

(350)

ALWAYS REMEMBER: From the time you are born, 'till you ride in a hearse, things are never so bad that they couldn't be worse! If you don't believe this, take a good took at your wife!

(351)

A New Yorker sent his wife, and his daughter Rebecca, to Miami Beach to try to find Rebecca a husband. They returned after only 10 days, but with no husband. He asked them why they returned so soon and his wile said, "We had to come back because there was an epidemic." The old man, alarmed, said, "What kind of epidemic." She replied, "it was clip." The daughter interrupted her and said, "No, Mama, It was the clap!" And her mama screamed, "Clip, clap, pip, pap, sip, sap, What's the difference, We BOTH GOT IT !"

(352)

"I'm in love with my horse, " The nervous young man told his psychiatrist. "Nothing to worry about," the psychiatrist consoled. "Many people are fond of animals. As a matter of fact, my wife and I have a dog we're very attached to." "But, doctor," continued the troubled patient, "I feel physically attached to my horse." "Hmmm," observed the doctor. "Is it male or female ?" "Female, of course !" The man replied curtly. "What do you think I am queer ?"

(353)

I took her in the morning ... And once again at noon.... I took her after super Before would be too soon... I took her once at bedtime... Again at half past three... It sure is getting tiresome ... Taking Lassie OUT TO PEE!

(354)

"Get undressed" the psychiatrist tells the young woman patient. "Take off everything and get on the couch." Confused, she follows orders. The shrink whips It out and hops aboard. Ten minutes later, he slides off. "Okay," he says, slipping his pants back on, "my problem is solved. Now let's consider yours.'

(355)

A husband stumbled into bed about three a.m., drunk as a loon, and fell fast asleep. when he woke up just before dawn, he looked down and exclaimed, "There's three pair of feet in this bed !" His wife snapped, "You drunken fool, you're seeing double!" He said, "Oh," and squinted, but it still looked like six feet, so he walked around to the foot of the bed and counted, "One... two....three.... four ...you're right, dear ! There's only two people there, and boy, I sure am snoring!"

(356)

They were doing some remodeling around her house, and a wolfish workman told our girl Vicki, "I keep hearing about that cat of yours... when are you gonna invite me to pet your pussy ?" Vicki smiled sweetly and answered, "I also have a donkey in my back yard. Why don't you walk around behind and kiss my ass ?"

(357)

A fellow taking a sex survey called up one of the husbands who had filled out his questionnaire and said, "Sir, there's a discrepancy in your answers. Under 'Frequency of Intercourse', you've put 'Twice a week', while your wife wrote, 'Several times nightly,' " The man replied, "Yes, that's right, but only until we get the second mortgage on our house paid off. . ."

(358)

Aunt Molly, who always smoked a pipe, was on her way down the mountain to sell a rooster, when she noticed a young bull trying very hard to carry out his duties with a willing heifer. After several attempts, he finally made it, and then fell to the ground. Aunt Molly exclaimed, "Die, damn you ... you've made me bite my pipe stem in two and choke my rooster to death !"

(359)

A boy and girl were spending their wedding night in an upper berth, and the amorous groom had set his traveling alarm clock to go off every hour on the hour. Each time it would ring, he would cuddle up to his bride and whisper, "Come on, baby. I'm ready for another taste of my little hot chicken." The fellow in the lower berth stood it for a while, but just about dawn he could take no more, so he hollered up to them, "Listen, folks, I wish you'd either shut off the oven timer or put a lid on your roaster. I can't get to sleep with that gravy dripping all over me!"

(360)

Stud and Lucy were riding along on his motorcycle, when she became real cold and turned her jacket around for warmth. Then Stud got so cold his glasses fogged, and he piled It up on a bridge railing. When he came to, he asked the ambulance driver, "Where's my bride? How is she?" The man answered slowly, "She was okay, until we moved her tits back around where they belonged."

(361)

After stopping his car on a deserted section of country road, the young man turned to his date and made some rather predictable advances. "Just a minute," the girl declared, pushing him away. "I'm really a prostitute and I have to charge you fifty dollars." After he reluctantly paid her, they made love. Later, the man sat silently at the wheel. "Aren't we leaving ?" the girl asked. "Not quite yet," the fellow said. "I'm really a cabdriver - and the fare back is fifty dollars."

(362)

An attractive young buyer for a department store was having coffee with her assistant and complaining about her fiancé's extraordinary sexual appetites. "I barely have the strength to come to work in the morning," she murmured. "And now that he's on his vacation, things will probably get worse." "How long is he off?" the assistant inquired. "It varies," she replied. "But usually it's just long enough to smoke a cigarette."

(363)

A Woman ran into the police station and said, "I've been raped!" The desk sergeant asked, "Where did it happen?" So she pulled up her skirt and showed him.

(364)

I think I've finally cured my husband of coming home in the wee hours of the morning," the wife proudly announced on New Year's Day. "Last night, when I heard him fumbling downstairs, I yelled: "Is that you, Harold?" "How has that cured him?" questioned her friend. "His name is Charles."

(365)

Debbie the Office Idiot says she accidentally dropped a birth control pill in the Xerox machine, and now it won't reproduce any more.

(366)

The dazzling young thing was strolling down the street in skin-tight hip huggers, when a curious bachelor approached and said, "Excuse me, miss, but I can't help asking - how in the world does anyone get into those pants?" "Well," she replied demurely, "you can start my buying me a drink"

(367)

The cute young teen age baby-sitter was changing the kids diaper and discovered his little talleywhacker was standing up stiff as a board. She turned to the Mother, who was on her way out the door, and said, "Take a look at this He is exactly like his Dad !" I bet you are wondering if the Mother canceled her plans to go out !

(368)

REMEMBER TO WRITE THIS IN THE NEXT BIRTHDAY CARD YOU SEND...The sun may kiss the butterfly ....The dew may kiss the grass A janitor may kiss the Motel Maid and you may kiss Another year Goodbye!

(369)

The host of the party asked a cute, sexy broad, "Would you like a cocktail?" She turned red with embarrassment and replied, "Well I'll be damned, how in the world did you know my last name was TAIL?"

(370)

Then there was the one about the brides Father who went to the Men's Room at the Wedding reception. When he returned to the main room, all the guests noted that he had forgotten to zip up his fly and his "talleywhacker" was swinging from side to side. One of the guests informed him of the situation and as he reached down to pull up the fly, he said so all could hear, "Well I'll be go to Hell, that's just like my wife, she never puts anything back after she has used it!"

(371)

The drunk was supposed to meet his buddy Richard at the bar but the buddy was already an hour late. The drunk decided maybe he should make a phone call to see if everything was all right. Richard's wife answered and the drunk proceeded to ask, "IS DICK IN ?" The wife replied, "Who are you trying to kid, Do you think I would answer the phone if it was !"

(372)

IT'S A TRUE FACT... Men do make a lot of passes at girls who are in a hurry to drain their glasses!

(373)

CLASSIFIED AD IN YOUR LOCAL PAPER..."PREGNANT GIRL WISHES TO MEET MAN IN NEED OF QUICK TAX EXEMPTION ! She received over 50 letters and at least a hundred phone calls!

(374)

After five years in an enemy prison, a POW wrote his wife, "When I open the door and see you standing there, I'm only going to ask one question.... period? And you'd better say no."

(375)

An old man went to the Social Security Office to apply for benefits. The clerk asked to see his birth certificate. He told her, "I ain't never had one. I was born in a small town where everybody knew who everybody was, and nobody ever asked anybody to prove it." She said, "In that case, take off your shirt." He did. She looked him over and decided, "You have gray hair on your chest and underarms, so you're old enough for benefits. Go on home and wait for your checks to come. " He went home and told his wife what had happened. She said, "Silly ass, you should have dropped your pants, too. You could've gotten total disability!"

(376)

A fellow was walking around the office handing out cigars. Someone asked, "Did your wife have a baby today?" He answered, "Better than that, she's gonna let me start one tonight!"

(377)

Grandma Lutz was talking to her young granddaughter, "You be very careful around that dummy Billy Blitz. I knew his grandfather when I was your age. It was at our high school graduation ball where I let him have a dance. He waltzed me off behind some bushes, held up a dollar bill, and told me, 'You see this buck? Some boys bet me two of these that I couldn't get in your pants. Help me win, and you can have this one for your cut.' That sounded fair, so I shucked my bloomers. He picked'em up, put'em on, ran away... and I never saw him, the money, or those underdrawers again!"

(378)

The husky trucker told the flirty little waitress, "I had the wildest dream about you and me last night. It was so real, I'd have sworn you were right there under me." She laughed, "in that case, Big boy, you'd better high tail it out of here and get a penicillin shot!"

(379)

A breeder was transporting his prize stallion around the countryside, renting it out to farmers with mares, for what your grandmother used to call "Immoral purposes." One little boy watched the action and asked what they were doing it for. His father explained, "To get little horses." The child squealed with delight, "NOW I KNOW why Uncle Homer comes to see Mama!"

(380)

Helen and Homer sat on a park bench locked in a passionate embrace. A man came along and sat down quietly beside them, but they didn't care. Then Homer noticed the man making hand signs. "What does that mean? " he asked. The man replied, "I'm not talking to you," so Homer went on about Helen's business. Then he saw the man tap Helen's shoulder. This was too much, so he yelled, "What in the hell do you want ?" The man retorted, "Butt out, Mister, this doesn't concern you. I just want to ask my wife for the house key."

(381)

A married man was having quite a few shots at Peacock Lounge. Finally the bartender asked what was wrong. He groaned, "My wife said she wasn't fulfilled at home, so she took a job. " The bartender consoled, So what ? Lots of women are doing that." The drinker yelped, "Yeah... but at a WHORE HOUSE ?" After a strangled silence, the bartender managed to say, "Well, at least you know for sure whether she sleeps around or not.   " The man moaned, "It isn't what I know that got me in Dutch. It's the place I got laid twice a week !"

(382)

"And what's more, Alice," the furious physician hollered as he slammed the front door, "You're a lousy lay !" Later, after completing his morning rounds, the doctor decided to drive by the house to apologize to his wife for his morning outburst. Not finding her in the kitchen or the living room, he glanced Into the bedroom, only to find her in bed with another physician. " what the hell is going on here ?" he demanded. "Well, after what you said this morning, dear," his wife explained," I decided to get a second opinion."

(383)

And then there was the one about the two drunks talking about their kids ... one said, "The other day my daughter came up to me and said, "I almost got in a fight at school today. Some boys called me a virgin, and !'m not." Well, I almost crapped ... after all, she's only ten. But I asked very carefully " What do you mean by that ? " With considerable pride in her voice, she answered, "Mommy already told me I'm a Sagittarius."

(384)

As they kissed good night in the hallway, the young man pleaded, "Can't I just step inside for a cup of coffee before the long drive home ?" The lady replied, "No, because after you drank, I know what you'd do." He persisted, "No, no, I wouldn't." She pouted, "You would, too. . . you'd reach in your pants and haul out a cigarette ... and I don't allow smoking in bed."

(385)

The first graders were supposed to draw pictures of what they wanted to be when they grew up. Little Johnny sketched a boxer with his fist raised, after he had knocked the other fighter 10 feet in the air and over the ropes. The teacher said, "Very good. You want to be a champion prize fighter." Johnny sneered, "Heck no, I want to be the one who's knocked up. Poppa said a high school girl got that way, and the principal paid her $5,000 to keep her mouth shut."

(386)

At a scoundrels' funeral, the preacher said, "Before we throw the dirt on this lying, cheating, stealing, dog-kicking polecat, will someone say a few kind words about the dear departed ?" There was total silence. The minister implored, "Come now, surely someone knows something good about this mother-beating sidewalk spitter ?" Still no one answered, so the reverend made a final plea. A little old woman stood up and timidly said, "He was damn good at sex and paid me at least a hundred a week!"

(387)

A lady sat down on the buss near a man who was holding two babies. "What lovely children," she gushed, "are they boys or girls ?" He said, "Hell, I don't know ... they're not mine. I'm just a poor, hard-working birth control pill salesman, and these are two complaints I'm taking back to the factory."

(388)

Momma took her little seven-year old daughter out of the bath and handed her to Daddy, who said, "You look so sweet, I could kiss you all over!" She answered, "Not unless you've got a bag of candy, like the nice old man who lives next door."

(389)

A stranger at the high school asked a sophomore boy, "How do you get to the principal's office ?" The kid suggested, "You could play hooky or cheat on exams... but my usual way is to goose a teacher."

(390)

In a small, rural town in Tennessee, we found an old cemetery with the following inscribed on a tombstone - .."ONCE THE COUNTRY'S FINEST SPREAD... BUT NOW SHE LAYS HERE, COLD AND DEAD!"

(391)

A mother was entertaining her bridge club when her little 5-year-old daughter rushed into the room and shouted, "Mama, Mama, there's a stranger up stairs in bed with the maid! The mother excused herself, saying she would look into the situation. As she started to climb the stairs, the little girl laughed and said, "APRIL FOOLS, MAMA ... IT'S ONLY DADDY!"

A little boy had hit his thumb with a hammer and was saying a few appropriate words, when the preacher walked up and said, "Son, when you curse like that, it makes cold chills run up and down my spine." The kid replied, "You should have heard what Mama said last night when Daddy "pooped" and then he pulled the sheet over her head ... I guarantee - you would have frozen to death!"

A camera crew was filming some of those on-the-spot, off-guard TV commercials, and their opening gimmick was for the emcee to insult every person he talked to and get their reactions.. "Because with "Intiment Spray" deodorant, folks, people will like you no matter WHAT you do" . . so he accosted one couple coming out of a hotel dining room and told the man, "Sir, your wife is the ugliest woman I've ever seen." The fellow replied, "Yes, I know. That's why I shack up with THIS lady."

Dick Hammer got out of bed one morning and drove down to the all-night drugstore to make an emergency purchase. A few minutes later, hearing the front door open and close, his wife called out, "Did you bring the rubbers ?" There was a nervous cough, and then a strange man's voice answered, "Yes, I did. But I think you ought to know, I'm not your regular milkman!"

Bob Adams complained to Zeke Buffet, "I think my wife's up to her old tricks. When supper was late last night, she said it was because she'd spent the afternoon over at your house with your wife." Zeke inquired, "What makes you think she didn't ?" Bob groaned, "She couldn't have... I was over at your house with your wife."

(396)

Hey fellows, how about getting some business cards printed up like this for your next visit to a bar ? "My Dear Young Lady: I'm kind of the 'shy type', and this is really most embarrassing for me, but would you think it too forward of me to invite you over for a 'get-together' luncheon, or perhaps tea? It would be just swell, talking to you about where you're from, discussing the weather and everything ... then we could have sex !"

(397)

When the bar cutie approached a young virile looking customer with her wares, he told her, "No, thanks. I'm saving myself for the girl I love." She said, "That's commendable, but isn't it awfully hard on you?" He replied, "No, not really. But it does bother my wife a little.

(398)

"HOMER" said the farmer's wife, "You been slopping hogs for two years now and ain't washed up yet. It's getting so I can't tell the difference between you and them." The next day Homer came running home, panting loudly, pants ripped open, and scratched all over. "Sarah," he yelled, "put a bar of soap on the shopping list. That old boar can't tell the difference neither!"

(399)

The 8th grade teacher asked an overgrown boy to spell date. He answered, "D-A-T". She said, "That's fine so far, but what's at the end of it?" He grinned, "A piece of tail, I hope."

(400)

A Marine and a Sailor were trying to meet the same girl, and the Marine was winning out, until the Sailor mentioned that the Marine's might be bigger, but he didn't have two. "Haven't you wondered," he asked, "why we wear these double-buttoned pants?" So the girl went off with the Sailor, and after several moments of pleasure, she put it back in and asked to see the other one. Opening the second set of buttons, he proceeded to bring out a sloppy and dangling one. She exclaimed, "Oh, my goodness, was it in a wreck?" The gob said, "No, it just pouting because it wasn't first."

(401)

Are you a football fan ? Did you ever stop to think that football is the nastiest game in the world ? First of all, the quarterback stands with his hands in the center's crotch and dispenses the balls; they're forever patting each other on the butt; and the stadium announcer adds to the effect with gems like, "Making it through a tight hole," and "Now they are really banging the receivers !" Maybe this is the reason that some wives like to watch football!

(402)

NO SCENT OF SEX.. .1 took my girl into the woods, A hidden spot I found. The blanket that I brought along ....Was spread upon the ground. When we began to make with love... My shaft was-quickly sunk. And then we were in trouble For towards us came a skunk. Before we could unwind ourselves He struck us with his phew. Just mention woods again to me And I'll say 'up yours too'!

(403)

Mrs. Peters, who is in town shopping, is supposed to meet her husband, Bob, in front of the courthouse at 1:00. Well, it gets to be 1:30, and he doesn't show. So she goes to look for him. He's not in the hardware store, and he isn't at the Elks Club. She sticks her head in at the door of the barbershop and asks, "Bob Peters here ?" "No, ma'am. Just cut hair."

(404)

A bride-to-be was opening her wedding presents and found one big beautiful wrapped package marked, "Wear this on the first night, and you'll be sure to please him. " She dug excitedly through the tissue paper. The package was empty.

(405)

Three ants met on a navel and decided to explore the surroundings. The first went up, the second went down, and the third ant went around. When they got back, the first ant said, "I went over two huge mountains, each of which was capped by a round peak." The second ant said, "I went along a ditch, but I didn't see much, because I got tangled up in the underbrush and almost fell into a hole." The third ant said, "You guys were lucky. I wound up in a cave, and a BIG BROWN GRUB WORM chased me out!"

(406)

Listen my children, and you shall her ....Of the midnight ride of a bottle of beer ... It goes down your throat and around your guts ... And comes out the spout just above your nuts.

(407)

ADVICE TO HUSBANDS: Do you tire of hearing your wife plead a headache when you're horny ? Next time she does it, retort, "Damn it, that's just what my secretary said!" You won't make her give you any loving, but at least she'll be able to offer a more interesting excuse for turning you down.

(408)

A rumpled little man carries two huge suitcases Into the Cancer Fund. "I have a million dollars to donate," he announces. "Where would a guy like you get that kind of cash ?" the official asks. "I'm a men's room attendant at the Waldorf. Every time a rich man comes to piss, I sneak up behind him with my switchblade, grab his balls and say, "Give me $10,000 for the Cancer Fund or I cut'em off." So now, in this suitcase, I have a million dollars." "Amazing But what's In the other case ?" "Well, not everybody gave."

(409)

As they left the cafe, Kellie whispered to Mike, "You sure gave that waiter a good tip! " Mike whispered back, "Not as good as the tip he gave me... my wife was coming in the other door."

(410)

A funeral parlor was having such bad business that it converted the back half of the building into a House of Massage. Now the sign out front reads, "MASSAGE AND FUNERAL PARLOR... There's No Stiff We Can't Handle."

(411)

HER FIRST TIME ? I climbed between the fresh, white sheets...On this, our wedding night...My bride slipped in the other side.... And then turned off the light.... I asked her why the darkness..... why be so shy with me..... She said, "I cannot bear to watch me giving it away for free!"

(412)

My Daddy was the butcher...My Mommy was the meat.... And I'm the little weenie.....the two cooked up so neat.

(413)

Every time Mike had sex with his wife, she would keep him awake the rest of the night by moaning, "More love, more love . . ." One dark night, he decided to give her what she wanted, so he called up a bunch of.' friends to sneak in one at a time and "spell" him. Then, just to see how passionate she really was, he trained his pet chimp to keep score on the wall, making a chalk mark for each bout. The flash light of morning found plies of very tired men sprawled and stacked all over the house all petered out, while Mike's wife writhed on the bed crying, "More love, more love..." The chimp sat on the floor nursing his strained wrist and chattering, "More chalk, more chalk. . ."

(414)

A stranger was trying to cash a check at the Cashmore Bank & Trust Co. The teller didn't want to take it because he didn't have much .identification. Suddenly a policeman walked up behind the man and shouted, "Hey, Joe Blow, you cog slugging so-and-so! ' The man told the teller, "See, this cop knows I'm who I say." She handed him a sheaf of bills, took the check, and he walked out chuckling. She then remarked to the cop, "It's lucky you came along to identify your friend." The cop shrugged, "I doubt if he'd call me his friend...I've arrested him for passing bad checks at least a hundred times."

(415)

The little old man is griping that he can't got it up any more. "I have no problems at all," says his equally ancient friend. "I eat a loaf of rye broad every day. " He's never heard the idea, but he's willing to try anything, so the man rushes to a supermarket and grabs a dozen loaves. At the checkout, the cashier warns, "Mister, if you buy this much bread at once it'll got hard." "Say," the old man asks, "how come everybody knows about rye bread except me ?"

(416)

One of the new spelling words was "BABY." A small girl raised her hand and asked, the teacher, could you have a baby?" The teacher claimed she could. The child asked, "Could my mother have a baby ?" Again the answer was yes. Then the wee miss wanted to know, "What about me ? Could I have one ?" The teacher laughed, "Not yet, you're much too young." A little boy In the back row said, "Boy that takes a lot of weight off my mind!"

(417)

My car has been stolen, oh pity my grief, my wife was inside it, I sure pity the thief.

(418)

A Woman's libber was recruiting housewives. A small boy answered the door at one house and said, "Mommy ain't home. She went to buy a gun." The Lib Lady inquired, "Did your Daddy tell her what kind of gun to buy ?" The boy replied, "No, I don't think so. In fact, I don't think he even knows she's gonna shoot him."

(419)

A young lad and his girlfriend decided to spend the weekend in a nudist camp. After about three hours, he asked her, "Honey, why do you lower your eyes when I say "I Love You ?" "Only to see if your telling the truth," she replied.

(420)

Speaking of nudist camps, they now have their own nude beaches and even the girl lifeguards are nude. The only thing bad about it is their rule that you can't drown without your wife's permission.

(421)

At the cocktail lounge two young ladies were talking and one says to the other, "You know, my boyfriend always takes a shower before and after we have sex. I didn't think it was funny, until his wife told me he does the same thing at home too.

(422)

Coming down the church steps on Sunday, this 87-year-old lady noticed a cute little freckle faced 4-year-old on the lawn, she walked over to him and said, "I sure wish I had a little boy just like you!" The little kid replied, "Then why don't you get knocked up like Mommy did!"

(423)

Did you hear about the little boy who was caught in the bathtub with a toothbrush In his hand ? He had tooth paste all over the bathroom. His Mom walked in and found him using that toothbrush on his little thing. She said, "Son what are you doing?" The boy replied, "I'm making sure it is clean, I don't want to get a cavity like my little sister!"

(424)

Two homeless men stopped at a farm house to see if they could get something to eat. The lady said she would be happy to fix them something if they would chop some wood for her fireplace. After about thirty minutes, the lady looked out the window and here was one of the homeless men doing cart wheels, back flips, hand springs and jumping up in the air at least ten feet. She went out the back door and asked the other man, "Gosh, that friend of yours is really great, he should be in show business. Did you know your buddy was an acrobat ?" He replied, "Gosh no, I guess it has something to do with me hitting him in the balls with this ax !"

(425)

Two hunters a little short in the brains department are deep in the woods when a naked blonde frolics past them. "Boy," says one hunter. Is she game ? The other hunter shoots her.

(426)

The suave guy picks out the best-looking girl at the singles bar and delivers his best line: "Sweet face, I'd really, really like to get into your pants." "Screw off.'" she zaps back.. "There's one asshole In there already, and that's plenty !"

(427)

The classified ad teased, "Impress your friends! Amazing device makes your penis appear twice as large as any you have seen.... maybe even larger! Rather than die of curiosity, we sent them ten bucks and what did he get? A magnifying glass.

(428)

Putt Downer: "We're having a party for virgins only. Can your wife come?"

(429)

My boss says I'd better not SCREW UP anymore..... it hurts his elbows to be on top.

(430)

Sign in Singles Bar. "Be grateful for Birth Control. Without It, you'd probably be married."

(431)

As he pulled off the highway with his new date, the young man asked hopefully, "Uh... how far do you go? " She obligingly admitted, "It really doesn't matter. Just so we can stop and have sex when we get there.

(432)

After sharing 50 years of friendship and a love of baseball with him, George was crushed to learn that his friend Harry was terminally ill. "Harry, buddy, I'm going to miss you, " George wept. Then, brightening he added, "But I've got to know if there's baseball in the afterlife. Promise you'll come back and tell me." "I promise," Harry croaked. Two weeks after Harry's death, George was awakened by a brilliant white light. "Harry? Is that you?' "It's me," Harry said. "Tell me. I have to know," George pleaded. "is there baseball in the afterlife?" "Well, I have some good news and some bad news." "What's the good news?" "There is baseball in the afterlife.' 'So, what could be bad?" "You're pitching Saturday."

"I'm exhausted," complains the first secretary. "I didn't get, to sleep until after four last night." "No wonder you're tired," says the second secretary. "two or three usually is all I can handle."

FEMALE AT NUDIST CAMP: "Welcome to Sunnyvale Naturalists Haven. I'm the director." MALE APPLICANT: "Very glad to meet you." FEMALE: "So I can see."

The wealthy sheep farmer is strolling the family property with an old pal. "And right there," he says, pointing to a spot by a stream, "is where I had my first sexual experience as a lad. Her mother was looking at us from behind that tree." "Her mother was looking at you? What'd she say?" "Not much - just baaaaa."

Mickey Mouse and Donald Duck are having a couple drinks at the bar, and Mickey is sobbing. "Did I hear right,?" quacks Donald Sympathetically. "Minnie Mouse had gone crazy?" 'No, no," says the Mick, "I said she's screwing Goofy!"

An old man and woman are driving on a raw, blustery night, when they feel something hit their car. They stop and discover they've nipped a baby skunk, who lies shivering in the road. The man carries the young animal to the car and gives It to his wife, saying, "Keep him warm until we get home- put him between your legs." "What about the smell ?" asks the woman. The old man replied, "He will get used to It just like I did !"

(438)

Bartender - "We're having a raffle for a poor widow. Can I sell you a ticket? Customer - "I'm afraid not. Even if I win, my wife wouldn't let me keep her."

(439)

Two young black women meet. "Where you been, Pearl?" "Twelve weeks in the hospital, honey." "What you have?" "Gonorrhea." "What? You doesn't stay no twelve weeks in no hospital for gonorrhea dese" days." "You does if you gives it to Leroy !"

(440)

Alimony, to most judges, is payment for services rendered during a marriage. In other words, It's the screwing you get for the screwing you got.

(441)

"How come your bulls breed so well and mine don't?" One farmer asks another. "I give them potency pills from the vet" is the reply. "Potency pills? What're they made of?" "damned If I know, but they taste a little like potato chips."

(442)

Have you ever noticed... All the officials of the NFL come running onto the field with their fly's open? I wouldn't say they were stupid, but all of them know that many, many times... they will have to count to Eleven ! "

(443)

Is that guy stupid? The only way he can count to twenty-one Is if he's naked.

(444)

A Toast to My critics: When I am In a sober mood - I worry, work and think. When I am in a drunken mood - I gamble, screw and drink. And when my moods are over - And my time has come to pass. I hope they bury me upside down - So the world can kiss my Butt!

(445)

"Did you ever hear a hormone?" "Only when I couldn't pay her."

(446)

A woman making the rounds at a cocktail party finally settles in front of a bleary - eyed but handsome young man. "What do you like most in a woman." she said in her sexiest voice. "Me." He replied.

(447)

"Ta". What the hell does that mean?" the man said, pointing at a man at the end of the bar. " It means 'thank you'. That guy's from Canada." "You know, boss, there's nothing In Canada but whores and hockey players." "My wife's from Canada." "Oh yeah, what team did she play for ?"

(448)

"My hearing aid stopped me from havin' so many kids." says one woman. "Now, how can that be ?' asks the other. "Every night In bed he asks, "Are we going to sleep or what ?' before I got my hearing aid, I'd always say 'WHAT' ?"

(449)

Then there was the midget lady who went into a bar and kissed everyone in the joint.

(450)

What's different about a whore, a mistress, and a wife? A whore asks, "Didn't you come yet?" A mistress asks, "Did you come already?" A wife says, "Sam, the ceiling needs painting!"

(451)

Bruce and Harvey, two gentlemen of the homosexual persuasion, are on the freeway when a giant trailer truck sideswipes their car. They swerve and graze the median, and by the time they can stop both sides of the car are fairly well mangled. "Tell him we'll sue!" screams Bruce. Harvey dashes over to the truck and looks up into the cab. "We'll sue!" he cries. "Yeah!" the driver sneers.' "Well, you can suck my............ I" Harvey goes back to Bruce In the car. " You know, sweetie," he says, "I think we can settle this out of court."

(452)

The farmer has more than a passing Interest in the shapely dairy maid, so to put her in the mood he brings, her to watch his best bull servicing a cow. "Boy," he offers unsubtle, "I'd love to be doing what that fellow is doing!" "Why don't you?" she replies. "It's your cow."

(453)

Three teenage sisters are leaving for their dates. "Bye mom," says the first, "I'm going with Lance - We're gonna dance." "Have fun.' says the mother. "Bye, mom," says the second, "I'm going with Moe - we're going to a show." "Enjoy it." says Mom. "Bye, Morn," says No. 3, 'I'm going with Chuck -" "Like hell !" Mom interrupts. "You're stayin' home !"

(454)

A gnarled old prospector is pushing his mule in vain try to get him to move. A young woman comes by and offers to help. She goes up to the mule and in a few seconds the beast takes off like greased lighting. "How'd ya do it, ma'am ?" the old guy asks. "just tickled his balls." she replies. "Well, try tickling mine, ma'am," the prospector says, "I gotta catch the bastard !'"

(455)

A horny young guy visits a sex therapist and cries, "I have no girlfriend and I just have to get some relief before I go crazy. I tell you, I'm going out of my mind. You gotta do something ! You gotta...." "Now, now." the doctor interrupts. "Get a hold of yourself."

(456)

The gas station attendant gets so fed up with clogged toilets that he puts up a sign in the John: DON'T PUT ANYTHING INTO THE TOILET BUT TOILET PAPER. So the first three guys who come in, crapped on the floor.

(457)

Why are bachelors thin and married guys fat? Bachelors come home, see what's in the refrigerator and go to bed. Married guys come home, see what's in bed and go to the refrigerator.

(458)

What's the difference between "Oooh !" and "Aaah !" Three inches.

(459)

"Where do babies come from, mama ?" "From the stork, honey." "Well, who knocks up the stork ?

(460)

"You're in such wonderful shape for your age," the reporter says to the gray-haired great-great granny on her hundredth birthday. "Have you ever been bedridden?" "Many times, sonny." the old lady replies dreamily. "And a couple of times in a buggy too."

(461)

A woman phones for an emergency appointment with her gynecologist. "My vibrator is stuck inside," She wails. "I'm sure the doctor will be able to remove it." soothes the nurse. "Oh, I don't want him to take it out." says the patient. "I just want him to replace the batteries."

(462)

Customer: "I'd like some Sex-lax, please." Pharmacist: "You mean Ex-Lax?" Customer: "No, I mean Sex-Lax. I don't have trouble GOING.."

(463)

The new bride complains to her mother that her husband isn't screwing her, just reading in bed and going to sleep. The older woman suggests a fancy nightgown, black garters and perfume. That night, more anxious than her daughter, she peeks into their bedroom, she sees the guy reaching for her daughters thing, figures things are fine, and leaves. Next day the daughter gripes again. "But I saw him reach for your thing," says the mother. "Big deal," grumbles the bride. "He was just wetting his finger to turn the page."

(464)

Then there was this society gal who was attending a party at a friends country estate. After about an hour she decided to go for a walk and get a little fresh air. Coming upon a nice, warm grassy field, she decided to lay down and watch the stars. She was almost asleep when she looked up and a cow was standing, straddled over her body. Half asleep she looked up at the cows udders and said. "O.K., you guys, please, only one at a time!"

(465)

The college professor was telling his first class of the day, "You all look so tired and sleepy this morning!" "It has been my experience that the best way to start the day is to exercise for about five minutes, take a deep breath and then finish with a good cold shower." "When this is all done, I really feel rosy all over"' From the back of the room comes this sleepy voice, "Tell us Professor, we want to hear more about Rosy!"

(466)

The cute little co-ed said to her date of the evening, "I'll tell you what, how about making this evening a "Dutch Treat" affair?" "You pay for dinner and drinks.....and the rest of the evening will be on me!"

(467)

Another sweet, little co-ed told her date, "Gosh, this evening at the Drive in Theater was both exciting and enjoyable. I wonder if the movie was any good?"

(468)

And then there was this couple meeting with the Marriage Counselor. The wife said, "It's not true what my husband told you about me not enjoying SEX." "I do enjoy it but this dummy husband of mine is a sex fiend and expects me to do it three or four times a year !"

(469)

One drunk says to the other, "You know, I just got a beautiful new Mink Coat for my Wife!" The other drunk replied, "God, I wish I could make a trade like that!"

(470)

The young Mother was out in the park pushing the baby buggy when a handsome astrologer walked over to her and said, "My, that is sure a beautiful baby, do you happen to know what sign he was conceived under ?" The young Mother blushed and replied, "I sure do, if I remember the exact words, I think it said "KEEP OFF THE GRASS !"

(471)

At a farm house way out in the boondocks, a baby was straining to be born. As the doctor entered the bedroom, he told the future father, "Wait out front. I'll call you if I need anything." After a few minutes, the medicine man hollered, "Bring me some pliers!" The husband yelped, "PLIERS ... WHAT FOR?" The doctor snarled, "Never mind that ... just bring'em!" The pliers were produced, but the doctor soon wanted a screwdriver. Then he screamed for a crowbar. The horrified farmer shrieked, "A CROW BAR ... WHAT ARE YOU DOING TO MY WIFE ?" The doctor bellered, "Don't waste time on fool questions! Fork over your damn crowbar!" The husband handed over his tool and waited in terror for the next request. It never came. Finally, the bedroom door squeaked ajar. The doctor slipped out, shook his head, and sadly sighed, "It's no use. We'd better rush her to the hospital. I can't open my little black bag."

(472)

While making her shopping list, the wife said to her husband, "Shall we have steak or chops?" Her husband, busy with a crossword puzzle, answered, "Yeah, okay." The wife asked, "Do you want pie or cake for dessert?" He grunted, "That's fine." The wife, now thinking out loud, mumbled, "Let's see, I gotta get some tooth paste, hand soap, douche powder. . ." Her husband interrupted, "Douche powder! How about getting that mint flavored like your sister uses!"

(473)

A wife was downtown shopping and happened to notice her husband coming out of a hotel with an attractive redhead. When she confronted him later, he blithely explained, "Hey, I was only holding the door for her. She's the cashier at the hotel coffee shop. I go there most every day for hotcakes and honey." The wife was skeptical, but she agreed to meet him there for lunch the next day. They both ordered hotcakes, but the waiter brought them to the table with a pitcher of syrup. The man looked up in surprise and asked, "Where's my honey?" The waiter replied, "Daisy?" She's at the cash register, same as always."

(474)

Bald men are often bothered by jokers rubbing a hand across the top of their hairless heads and saying, "This feels just like my wife's behind." You can silence such dumb bells with any of the following replies: "No, I believe her bottom's a bit smoother" . . ."Yes, EVERYONE says so." . . . "It doesn't' got petted as often, though," . . ."I don't think she shaves that close," or "But it smells nicer." Or you might run a hanky over your head as you mumble, "I knew there was something I forgot to wipe!" Dumb Bells.

(475)

Buster believed anybody would do anything for enough money. One day he told the preacher, "I'll give you a thousand dollars if I can sleep with your wife." The preacher thought it over for a while and agreed, "Okay. Be at my place tonight with the cash, and I'll let you." Buster came over that night, handed the preacher a fist full of greenbacks, and asked, "Where's your Wife?" The preacher replied, "She's already asleep. Go get in bed with her." Buster rushed to the bedroom, undressed, crawled under the covers, and started to wake the woman up. Suddenly the door creaked open. The preacher came in with a pistol, sat down in a chair by the bed, and said, "Okay, you paid a thousand dollars to sleep with my wife... so start sleeping!"

(476)

The husband came home late one night. When he opened the front door, a man rushed out, jumped into a car at the curb, and sped away. The husband went upstairs and asked his wife, "Who was that bastard ?" She replied, "At first I thought it was you. He undressed in the dark just like you, he foreplayed like you, he kissed me in all the same places you do, his equipment was the same size and he used it just the same way." The husband asked, "So how did you know it was somebody else?" She explained, "When we got through, he said, 'Lets do it again.' "

(477)

A farmer sat reading at the kitchen table by lamp light, while a midwife waited patiently at his wife's bedside. Suddenly the midwife shouted, "Bring the lamp! The baby's coming!" He trotted in and held the lamp while his wife was delivered ot a girl child, then headed back for the kitchen. Halfway down the hall, he heard the midwife scream, "Bring the lamp again! It's gonna be twins!" He held the lamp while a boy child was born, then returned to his reading. Moments later, the midwife shouted, "Bring back the lamp! Here comes another'" The farmer hollered, "Not on your life, lady! I think the damn light's attracting them!"

(478)

As they cuddled in the car, the young lady purred, "Wouldn't it be wonderful to change my name to yours?" The young man exclaimed, "Why in the world would you want people to call you Homer? "

(479)

The girls at the office had "Had it" - they voted to hang this sign in the company rest room, "Men, please pick up seat before hanging tool out, or we'll have it removed."

(480)

On an application for employment, this gal came upon the question, "What was your Mothers name before she was married?" The girl wrote, "I didn't have any Mother before she was married!"

(481)

DIZZY DEFINITIONS ... WHAT IS A ALARM CLOCK? It is an ideal wedding present for the couple who may find it hard when they get up in the morning! ALMOND JOY? It's a delicacy all the girls like to eat, because it's six inches long and has two nuts! ALIMONY? It's the screwing you get for the screwing you got! ASPIRIN TABLET? It's the world's most effective contraceptive pill; all you have to do is keep one between your knees! BAD GIRL? It's one who does something you and your girl friend never got caught at! BONER? It's newspaper slang for a blooper, where something serious comes out as humorous. Example: "Mr. and Mrs. Peter Burns off on their honeymoon!" BULL? It's a male bovine that, on a cold day, will always go into a barn and slip into a warm Jersey! ASTRONAUT FEVER? It's a Spaceman's disease ! They get it only when they can't get their missile up! CHERRY? It's something the groom gets on his wedding day, usually in his cocktail at the wedding reception! BANANAS & CUCUMBERS? The ideal diet for women. You won't lose any weight but you'll sure have a happy monkey!

(482)

At the wedding reception, the bartender put two cherries in the groom's Manhattan. He explained, "I think I should tell you that I was your wife's first boyfriend, so I owe you one!"

(483)

On the morning after the wedding, the groom woke up and noticed his new bride writing a letter. He asked her, "Honey, who are you writing to?" She replied, "My Mother and by the way..... is DISAPPOINTMENT spelled with one "S" or two?"

(484)

A catering service put up a new sign in front of their building. It read, "ARE YOU GETTING MARRIED, OR HAVING AN AFFAIR? LET US HELP YOU!

(485)

Homer loves to brag, he said, "I'm 78-years-old and I can still go at least three times in one night." His wife snickered, then added, "He sure can, even four times. . . to the bathroom!

(486)

Two men were brought into court for fighting. All the bystanders were on one man's side. The Other fellow pleaded, "Your Honor, I have no witnesses, but I had a right to hit that S.O.B.. He said my wife was the ugliest, dirtiest, smelliest, hairiest old whore in town." The judge replied, "Well, you should have some sort of a character witness. Can you bring your wife to court?" The man mumbled, "Er, uh ... Your Honor ... before I do . . . will it hurt my case if the guy is telling the truth?"

(487)

Clem and Clara were walking home through the woods. Clara said, "Clem, I have the feeling you want something." Clem protested, "No, Clara, I'm only seeing you safe to your house. I'm not one of those wolves." After a while longer, she said, "I still have this feeling you want some." He insisted, "You can trust me, I don't have anything bad on my mind." So they walked on in silence for a few minutes. Then Clara moaned, "Clem, this feeling is driving me nuts. Will you please take that big thing out so I can hold it!

(488)

"If you promise to be virgins until you are married," Dad announced to his three daughters, "I'll give you each a thousand dollars for a wedding gift." The 13-year-old spoke up immediately. "Wow, a thousand dollars!" she cried. "I'll promise!" The 16-year-old was a bit hesitant. "I'll try," she swore, "but my pants are getting awfully hot lately." Dad turned to ten-year-old Suzy, who had been listening with a bumfuzzled expression. "Do you know what I'm talking about?" he asked sternly. "Gee, Dad, I know what you mean," she whispered, "I just wish you had made this offer about 2 weeks ago!"

(489)

The traveling salesman waded through the mob of kids in the yard and started to knock on the farmers door. Then he noticed a man and a woman on the porch swing having sexual intercourse. Figuring they weren't in the mood to talk about milking machines, he went on to the next farm, where he remarked to the farmer, "Your neighbor down the road sure likes to make babies." The man replied, "I'll say! His wife's in the hospital now having their 12th, and my wife's over at his place helping out."

(490)

The harried stockbroker was suffering from insomnia, never got to sleep before dawn, then slept right through the alarm and so never made it to the office on time. Upon being reprimanded by his boss, he decided to consult a doctor. The doctor gave him some sleeping pills, and that night he fell asleep immediately and experienced a pleasant rest. in the morning, he awoke before the alarm rang, jumped out of bed and with new verve and vigor. When he arrived at his office promptly, he told his boss: "Those pills I got from my doctor really work I had no trouble at all waking up this morning." "That's nice," the boss replied, "But, where were you yesterday?"

(491)

A Texas millionaire went to one of New York City's more accommodating hotels and called room Service to send up a woman. He undressed and lay down on the bed. Several minutes later, a woman came In, looked at him, screamed, and ran Out Of the room. He called again, and the same thing happened. So he phoned room service a third time and said, "Would you send up one more woman? But tell this one not to turn on the light when she comes." Then he leaned back and relaxed. Ten minutes later, he heard something shuffling around the room, then he felt a pair of warm, moist arms encircle his neck, and heard a soft voice say, "You Texans sure are modest. You're not at all like the guys from New YYOORRKK!"

(492)

As Bill and Fred stood on the street comer, a gorgeous girl in a mini-skirt walked by, causing Bill's eyes to almost fall out of his head. Fred remarked, "She's a looker all right, but don't forget those five kids!" Bill gasped, "Surely that young thing doesn't have five children!" Fred said, "No, but you do . . ."

(493)

A young girl married an old fellow who could do nothing about it except play around and stick his finger up it occasionally, as she frequently complained to the young men hanging about the place. After two years of marriage, the girl became pregnant, and in due course was delivered of a bouncing baby boy. When she showed it to the old man he exclaimed, "How beautiful! And all handmade too!"

A SPECIAL POEM FROM YOUR AUTHOR

It's great to be a jokester, to sit up late at night, to scratch your wool and shoot the bull, and write, and write, and write! And it doesn't matter how you scrape your fingers to the bone...THERE IS SURE TO BE SOME OF YOUR READERS WHO SAY "I'VE HEARD THAT ONE BEFORE!"

(495)

A RECIPE FOR TURKEY DRESSING

2 cups bread crumbs
1/2 cup butter
1 Tsp. Salt
2 small onions
Celery to taste
2 cups popcorn (unpopped)

This recipe takes 5 hours to cook.   When popcorn pops, it will blow the turkey's ass clear across the room!!! Who eats it, anyway?

(496)

"I'm so tired," complained the pretty young actress to her friend. "Last night I didn't sleep until after three." "No wonder you're tired,' her friend replied. "Twice is usually all I need!"

(497)

At the local tavern two women were talking and one said, "When I was pregnant, the dummy who lives next door told his little boy my big tummy was only gas." After my baby was born, her kid saw my flat front and squealed, "Golly! I'm sure glad I wasn't' around when you let that poop!"

(498)

A BOY AT COLLEGE RECEIVED THIS LETTER ...

DEAR Mike,

I was thrilled by your invitation to come up next weekend and see your team play State! Also, I look forward to seeing the campus library and Pre-History Museum. I trust you'll make suitable sleeping arrangements, as you know I'm not the sort of person who *shacks up*.

Love, Helen

P.S. Just checked the calendar, and we'd better wait till the Miami game. I'll be on the rag next weekend.

(499)

Fat Bertha waddled into the Slimming Gym and told the masseuse, "You gotta help me. My husband gave me a present, and I can't get into it." The trainer promised, "Don't worry in a few weeks we'll hammer away enough blubber so your dress will fit. " Bertha pouted, "Who mentioned a dress? He gave me a Volkswagen."

(500)

A woman dialed the police station to request, "Cancel my report about the Peeping Tom. It was only a neighbor, it seems my husband told him to "Look in on me" while he was out of town!

(501)

Two tiny tots were looking at an abstract painting in the museum. One said to the other, "I don't know much about art, but I know if I made a mess like that, Mommy would change my diaper."

(502)

Two neighbor ladies talking over the back fence... One says, "My husband is so sweet. When we were first married, I used to miss those little bars of soap we'd been picking up at motels. But now every time he works late, he stops off and brings me home a couple of them and at least one bottle of shampoo!"

(503)

Grandpa Fudd used to pull it out and dangle it in front of the children, and they enjoyed it immensely, as most of them had never seen a railroad watch before.

(504)

Most people think that B.Y.O.B. on an invitation means "Bring your own bottle" or maybe "bring your own blonde," but my cheap neighbor always uses it when he invites me over for a back yard barbecue. He says it means 'Bring your own beef!"

(505)

You know they use a great deal of psychology in the hospitals these days. They never give out sleeping pills anymore. I heard one of the doctors tell the nurse, "When this patient wakes up, give him three quarts of hot enema. The poor guy slept for 13 days!"

(506)

Those TV commercials are always pushing headaches and how fast their particular brand works! "It's a big lie.. It takes a half an hour to get the top off the container and another half hour to get the damn cotton out!"

(507)

Buying merchandise by way of radio and television is a rip-off. I sent a radio station my check, for $4.95 and asked them to send me an album of "Oldies but Goodies." You know what I got ? A nude picture of Janet Reno!

(508)

SATURDAY NIGHT IN A COLLEGE TOWN !
That's the night the girls sow their wild oats!
When they get up Sunday morning, they pray for a crop failure!

(509)

There are three two-letter words that begin with "I" and they are a source of -much chagrin... they can make a man cry and make him want to die, when he hears those three words, "Is it in?"

(510)

The Family Planning Group was starting a drive for contributions to the public sperm bank. The first man they walked up to said, "No, I am very sorry, but I prefer giving the United Way!"

(511)

When they'd arrived at her apartment after a blind date, the girl asked, "Would you like to have a little drink,?" "I'd like to have a little - period!" said the boy, smiling. "You must have ESP" chirped the girl ... "how in the world did you know it was my time of the month?"

(512)

Have you heard about the aging star in those hard core skin flicks ? He arrived home completely worn, out. "Did you have a hard day at the studio, baby?" asked his girlfriend as she handed him a drink. "Yes, thank God. Anytime I don't have a hard day, I know they will replace me!"

(513)

Here's some good advice for women. If you have to criticize your man, do it like you were watering one of your favorite plants. Gently enough to encourage growth without destroying the root!

(514)

ANOTHER TOAST FOR YOU!

He who drinks gets drunk. He who gets drunk falls asleep. He who falls asleep gets no sex. He who gets no sex gets no child, so... let's all have a drink, and solve the population problem!

(515)

Girls, have you heard about the new bikini bathing suit that sells for $150 ? Boy, is it a "rip off." Know what it is ? "Two Band-Aids and a cork !"

(516)

Did you ever stop to think...? It's only at a nudist wedding where you can really tell who the best man is!

(517)

My friend came from Arcola, Illinois. It's the only town I know of where the population hasn't changed for over 20 years. Every time a baby is born, some fellow leaves town!

(518)

What is the most popular service provided by a Massage Parlor? Take away the "M" and "Age" in Massage and you'll have it!

(519)

Two farmers were visiting, the local town bar and one says to the other, "I was sure sorry to hear about your wife running off with your hired man." His friend replied, "Don't think anything about it, I was going to fire him anyway."

(520)

Then there was the one about the two drunks who decided to quit their jobs and go into business for themselves. One drunk says to the other, "Why don't we go into the whorehouse business?" He other drunk replied, "That's a great idea and you know something, we can run it by hand until we can afford some girls!"

(521)

Here's a question for you... 'What is found on a pool table and is also found in men's trousers?" Stop and think now! You are wrong! The answer is ... pockets !

(522)

An angel came down with a great big pail, and gave each bird and fish a tail. But, the tails ran out when she got to man, so, he has to get his wherever he can!

(523)

REMEMBER...When you used to do it all night long... now it takes all night to do it!

(524)

Then there was the bartender who was always singing "I'm forever blowing bubbles" to his customers. Then came the day when one of his drunk customers couldn't take it anymore and said, " I didn't even know you were going with her..."

(525)

Two drunks sat the bar bombed out of their mind and drinking their tenth martini...one says to the other, "Ish, Ish, my peter hanging out ?" His friend looked down, and said, 'No." The first drunk started crying and replied, "Wel-sh, Wel-sh, it auto be, I'm peeing! "

(526)

Two Jewish ladies are visiting when one says, "How do you like your condominium. ?" The other lady replied, 'Oh, they are all right I guess, but truthfully, the birth control pills are working all right!"

(527)

Did you hear about the guy who was dating a girl who worked for a finance company? He got a little behind with his car payments!

(528)

The young nurse remarked to her supervisor, "My mother tells me that women make the best doctors." The head nurse smiled and said, "That's sure right honey, I've had some damn good ones myself."

(529)

Dear Miss Mummers: "If you knocked up your grandmother, what kin would the baby be to you? Please hurry with the reply as my printer is waiting to run off the announcements?"

(530)

How about the married couple who wanted to improve their sex lives. The husband told his wife, "Darling, I've decided we can enhance our sex by doing it a new and different way. Starting tonight, we are going to do it back to back." His wife replied, "I really don't understand how either one of us will get any satisfaction by doing it that way." The husband says, "Oh yes we will, I have a surprise for you, tonight at 8:00, I have invited another couple."

(531)

Did you ever stop to think, it wasn't an apple in a tree that caused all the problems we have in this world.. It was a pear on the ground!

(532)

Girls, do you know how to really hurt the feelings of that egotistical moron you know ? All you have to say is, "Is it in?"

(533)

How do you become a stripper in a local bar? That's easy, you simply raise your right leg and then your left leg and between them both, you make your money!

(534)

Then there was the one about the little 7-year-old girl, out in the back yard playing with the neighbor kids. All of a sudden she ran to the back door of her house and said, 'Mama, can 7-year-old girls get pregnant?" Mother yelled from inside the house, "Of course not honey." With that, the little girl ran out into the back yard again and said, "OK fellows, under the porch, same game!"

(535)

Have you seen the new bumper length BUMPER STICKER? It reads...

"If you drink - don't park. Accidents cause people!"

(536)

Did you ever stop to think...one of the most expensive things in this world is a young girl who is free for the evening!

(537)

"Give me a kiss," the fellow ordered his cute little date. "You'll have to make me," she teased. "What the hell is your hurry," he protested "I just wanted to start out with a little kiss."

(538)

Speaking of a kiss, have you heard the new song being -played in all the college dormitories ? The title is "I USED TO KISS HER ON THE LIPS, BUT IT IS ALL OVER NOW."

(539)

Then, there was the sleepy new bride who couldn't stay awake for a second!

(540)

What are the two worst words in a marriage proposal? "YOU'RE WHAT?"

(541)

WANT AD

FOR SALE

Like new book on the rhythm method
or
will trade book for like new baby clothes

(542)

STANDARD SIGN FOUND IN EVERY ROOM OF A WHORE HOUSE.

"DON'T MAKE THE SAME MISTAKE YOUR FATHER DID....

PULL OUT!

(543)

HERE'S ONE TO MEMORIZE FOR YOUR NEXT PARTY

He got it in the kitchen,
He got in on a chair,
He got it on his fingers,
And rubbed it in her hair,
Now, dirty-minded reader,
You are making a mistake,
The thing he got was just
A slice of Happy Birthday cake!

(544)

The beautiful eighteen year old girl, sobbing quietly at the funeral service for her seventy-five-year-old husband, was overheard confiding to a solicitous neighbor: "We had such a happy marriage for the six months it lasted. Every Sunday morning he would make love to me, and he'd keep time with the church bells that summoned you all to the services." She sobbed a little, then said with rising animation, "and he'd still be alive today if it weren't for that damned fire engine that went clanging by!"

(545)

I knew our marriage wouldn't last long when my bride insisted that the wedding march be replaced with, " WHAT KIND OF FOOL AM I?"

(546)

Little Johnny was sent to the principle's office and was informed that P.T.A. did no stand for "Pat Teacher's Ass!"

(547)

Uncle Fud is much improved since he had his nuts removed...
Not only has he lost his desire, but he now sings tenor in the choir!

(548)

If the U.S. airlines want to increase their profits, all they have to do is insist that all male passengers be "strip searched" by their stewardesses. There would be a 100 percent increase in ticket sales!

(549)

What were the first words Eve said to Adam when she met him for the very first time? If you said, "That's a real hard one, you are absolutely correct!"

(550)

A good friend of ours points out that at cocktail parties, the men usually stand around getting stiff and the women are usually tight, but when they get home, they frequently find that neither is either.

(551)

Never make love on an empty stomach says a good friend of ours ... "take her out to dinner first!"

(552)

Did you hear about the two Burmese girls who were looking for a Manalay?

(553)

The man from Mars landed in Las Vegas and walked into a casino. He passed a slot machine that suddenly whirred noisily, then discharged a jack pot of silver dollars. The Martian looked closely at the machine and then said, "You know, you should stay home with a cold like that!"

(554)

"Give me a double whiskey!" the little boy yelled to the barmaid as he entered the show bar. "Do you want me to get in trouble?" she asked. The lad replied, "maybe later, but right row, I just want a drink!"

(555)

"Oh, Otis! You go up and down so smoothly No wonder your mom named you after an elevator!"

(556)

I'm writing a poem for my girlfriend, and it's got me all perplexed; I need one more word to make it end, do you know what rhymes with oversexed?

(557)

TELL IT LIKE IT IS!!
A small girl asked her mother, "Was I planned, or was I an accident?"
Mom replied, "Neither honey, you were a little booby trap I set to
catch your daddy!"

(558)

YOU WANT TO BE COOL? The next time you're in bed with a
women and her husband walks in at the worst possible time, simply
say, "Just a minute, buddy... I'm almost finished!"

(559)

Two drunks visiting the courthouse, and one asked the other, "That
man over there, is he a judge?" The other drunk replied, "Yes, but not
a very good one. Have you seen that pig he married?"

(560)

AD IN THE CLASSIFIEDS...

"How would you feel if you got pregnant. and couldn't get an abortion,
and had to live with six children you didn't want, and couldn't feed.
Well, that's how my pussy feels! Please, please phone now for a free
kitten!"

(561)

"There's going to be a new baby in our family," little Johnny proudly
told his school mates. One day his mother let him put his ear to her
stomach so he could feel the baby move. Next day when Johnny went
to school, he sadly announced to the others, "Remember that baby I
told you we were going to have? Well, you can forget it. My mother
ate it."

(562)

A 15-year-old girl, on her initial visit to the prenatal clinic, was told by the examining physician that she was pregnant. "When did this happen to you?" he asked, "Well," she replied, "it might have been one night when my parents went to the movies . . . " and then she added, "I'd have gone too, but the picture was for adults only."

(563)

They had a big tornado up in Snyder, Oklahoma, and one of the old settlers remarked, "I peeked out of my storm cellar at the height of the blow and saw my old cow give birth to the same calf three times! "

(564)

Scientists have determined that the average time of intercourse is four minutes. The average number of strokes per minute is nine, making the average intercourse consist of thirty-six strokes. Since the average length is six inches. The average girl receives 216 inches, or 18 feet, per intercourse. The average girl does it about three times a week, fifty weeks out of the year, and 150 times 18 makes 2,700 feet, or just a little over half a mile. So, girls, if you're not getting your half mile every year, why not let the man who bought this book help you catch up?"

(565)

CONTRACEPTIVE

An article to be worn on every conceivable occasion !

(566)

The honeymooners were checking out of the hotel. "What's this item, $100 for meals?" the groom asked the clerk "I never came down for dinner. I'm on my honeymoon." "We're on the European plan here" "It was there for you. If you didn't use it, it's not our fault !" "Well then, we're even," said the bridegroom. "Because you owe me $100 for making love to my wife." "I never touched your wife !" exclaimed the clerk. " Look, it was there for you. If you didn't use it, it's not my fault."

(567)

"I'm going to have a little one"
Said the girl, so gay and frisky.
When her boyfriend up and fainted,
She told him she meant whiskey!

(568)

A traveling salesman in the most rural part of Oklahoma sees a boy screwing a huge jack rabbit.....A while later he spies a bearded codger, about 85, sitting on a fence playing with himself. He pulls over and says to the old-timer, "You Okies are something else. First I see a kid screwing a rabbit and now I see you with your pecker in your hand." "What do you want? " asks the old guy, "You think I can catch jackrabbits at my age?

(569)

NEWS PAPER ADVERTISEMENT

Will whoever took my wallet at last Friday's football game, please return my identification cards and photos. You will keep the money, of course, and I have already canceled the credit cards. As for the contraceptives, you might as well keep those too. They'll make a nice gift for your parents, should they ever decide to get married."

(570)

A traveling salesman explained to the divorce judge, "My job keeps me on the road from Monday to Friday, so naturally when I'm home, I try to make up for lost time. Last Sunday morning, as my wife and I exercised the squeaky bed springs, someone in the next apartment banged on the wall and shouted, "Can't you AT LEAST stop that racket during the weekend? "

(571)

An advertising executive phoned his wife, who was visiting at her parents' horse ranch. The switchboard operator got the calls mixed up and plugged him in on a stable hand who was reporting to the trainer about a new filly. The ad man asked, "How is my little treasure this morning?" The stableman boomed, "Just beautiful! Four men have mounted her already, and she can hardly wait to take on another!"

(572)

A married man was planning a fishing expedition. He told his wife, "Pack my silk pajamas. They'll feel good while I lie under the stars at night and listen to the wilderness." When he returned from the trip, he asked, "Why didn't you pack my silk pajamas?" She said, "I did. I put them in your tackle box."

(573)

Love makes the world go round...and your girlfriend too, if she misses her pill!

(574)

The college girl had invited some sorority sisters to visit at the farm during spring vacation. Before her guests arrived, she went to her mother asked, "You know how Paw always shows off the crops and brags about spreading manure to make them grow? Couldn't you persuade him to call it 'fertilizer'? " The mother answered wearily, "My child, do you have any idea how long it took me to get him to say 'MANURE'?"

(575)

THE TRUCKER SONG

If a truck driver knocks knocks
Girls, don't answer at all
He hasn't just come
For a kiss in the hall
And once you have taken
A ride on his truck,
You'll be rocking a cradle
And cursing your luck!

(576)

After a buying trip to New York, the small town clothing merchant confessed to his partner, "I dated a sexy model, but she priced herself out of the market. When she asked me for $ 100, I couldn't get it up!"

(577)

"Well.," said the farmer to the traveling salesman, "We don't get many visitors this far off the beaten track, but since your car broke down, you'll have to sleep either with the baby or in the barn." "I'll take the barn," said the travel man, envisioning the baby wetting him in his slumber. The next morning, a beautiful young girl walked into the barn to milk the cow. "Who are you?" asked the salesman. "I'm the baby of the family," she replied. "Who are you?" "I'm the dumb ass who slept in the barn!"

(578)

A ventriloquist at a farm was amazing the neighboring farm hands with his talents. He threw his voice so it sounded like a horse standing nearby said, "Hello there, Zeke!" Then he made the cow moo: "Oh, my aching teats!" He was looking thoughtfully at a flock of sheep nearby when one of the hired hands shouted, "Listen, if that little ewe at the end says anything, she's a goddamn liar."

(579)

Max was 85. "You gotta help me, doctor," he pleaded. "I got a date with a 23 year old secretary and I want to be sure that I'm able to perform. Can you give me something to pep me up?" The physician smiled, wrote out a prescription, and had the old duck fill it. Later that night, out of curiosity, he telephoned him. "Did the medicine help any?" asked the MD. "It was great!" replied the old man. "I've managed three times already!" "Swell," said the doctor. "What about the girl?" "Oh, she hasn't gotten here yet!'

(580)

Two Michigan State football stars, Tom and Greg, took two pretty coeds out for a ride in their car. They drove twenty miles out from the campus and parked on a lonely stretch of road. "Now we're gonna proceed with this hereafter date, " announced Tom. "What's a hereafter date-?" asked one of the girls. "If you aren't here after what we're here after, you're gonna be here after we're gone. "

(581)

When Danny was in the hospital, he had a day nurse and a night nurse. In the afternoon he rested.

(582)

A pretty airline stewardess walked into a bar wearing a pair of tight fitting slacks. You could see every ripple of her flesh as she sashayed up to a stool and sat down. A fellow, right beside her, said, "Hey honey, how do you get into those pants?" "Well," said the stewardess, "you can start by buying me a martini!"

(583)

A 12-year-old boy accused of fathering a child was brought before the judge. The lawyer, in order to prove the absurdity of the charge, unzipped the youngster's pants. "Your honor," said the lawyer, "look at this tiny organ, this immature equipment. How could a boy father a baby with this little undeveloped..." "Hey, mister," whispered the boy, 'you better quit stroking me like that or we're gonna lose this case!"

(584)

The 60-year-old woman went to her doctor and asked for a prescription for birth control pills. "But you don't need them at your age," he said. She went on to explain that she had tried some recently and now found that she couldn't sleep without them. "But birth control pills have no tranquilizing agent in them," the doctor informed her. "Well I don't know what they have or what they don't have in them, but I give them to my daughter before she goes out each night, and I'm telling you, doctor, I sleep much, much better!"

(585)

"We're going to have a wonderful time tonight, dearest," said the young man to his date as he greeted her in the living room of her parents' home. "I have three tickets to the theater." "But why do we need three tickets?" asked the truly voluptuous young lady. He said they aren't for us...they're for your mother, father and sister! "

(586)

The young bride was having her new house decorated and, while changing into something suitable for her afternoon bridge club, she noticed what appeared to be her husband's hand print on the wall in the bedroom that had been freshly painted the day before. She slipped into a filmy but adequate covering and, going to the head of the stairs, called down to the painter who was now working in the living room. "Pardon me, but would you like to come up here and see where my husband put his hand last night?" she said. "I'd love to lady," replied the painter, "but I've got to get done with this painting first."

(587)

"Please, I'd like a leave of absence," the about-to-become-obviously pregnant airline stewardess told her supervisor. "Why?" she was asked. "It's because I've had - well - a sort of accident," answered the girl. "What was the cause of this accident?" pursued the supervisor, "Was it job related?" "In a manner of speaking," sighed the stewardess, "You might put the cause down as plot error."

(588)

It was at a homecoming dance that the handsome, but painfully shy young man approached the popular sexpot and mumbled, "Gee, I don't mean to be fresh, but if you, you know, danced with me, it would be quite a feather in my cap." "Let's split and go to a motel, " twinkled the girl, "and I'll make you an Indian chief."

(589)

Two housewives were discussing the TV special production of 'The God father" "It must be a terrible thing, Bertha," remarked one of them, "to wake up with a horse's head in your bed." "I should be so lucky," sneered Bertha. "With my Harry, it's a horse's ass.

(590)

The high school cheerleader confessed to the kindly old priest that she'd been having sexual intercourse with her boyfriend in the front seat of his car every night for the past two months. "Don't you think you've been doing something wrong?" admonished the cleric gently. "I guess you're right,' she mumbled thoughtfully. "Maybe it would be more comfortable in the back seat."

(591)

When the man and wife got into bed for some lovemaking one night, instead of responding, she complained for 30 minutes about economic conditions in the world. "Everything is going up," she wined. "The price of food, the cost of clothes, the beauty shop. I'd be happy if just one thing would go down." Came the sleepy reply, "you just got your wish!"

(592)

During a brief lull in an exhausting night of passionate lovemaking, the tireless young man made several overtures to continue. "Oh, I can't," signed his date contentedly. "I'm on strike." "So am I," he answered, "just as soon as I can get a raise, we'll both go back to work,"

(593)

A bachelor businessman we know declares that no matter how many positions formally held by men are taken over by women, there will always be one opening that only a man can fill.

(594)

Four nurses had decided to play practical joke on a new intern to test his sense of humor, and met to report what each had done. "I stuffed cotton in his stethoscope," said the first nurse. "I changed the names on some of his charts," added the second. "I was more personal," giggled the third girl. "I found a package of contraceptives in his desk drawer and put a pinhole in every one of them." The fourth nurse fainted.

(595)

Closing her book, the little girl asked her mother, "Mommy, do all fairy tales begin with 'Once upon a time . . . ?" "No, dear," her mother whispered, "sometimes they start with 'Sweetheart, I'll be working a little late at the office tonight . . . "

(596)

A free-loving girl was filling out an employment application and came to the line marked "Sex," followed by the usual little boxes, "M" and "F". She checked "F" and on the line below, added: "I've been averaging about three times a week!"

(597)

A sex researcher was questioning a pretty matron about her amorous habits. "Do you ever have intercourse in the daytime?" he asked. "Yes," she revealed, "about three times a week." "And do you and your husband talk to each other at those times?" "Well, no," she admitted, "but we could if I wanted to - I know his office phone number."

(598)

It was to be the student pastor's first service and he was quite nervous. The kindly old pastor said he knew, something that might help him through it: "Mix some gin with the water in the pitcher." When the young fellow returned to the rectory after the service, he asked the pastor how he had done. "Not badly, although there were a few slips," said the older man. "During the invocation, you referred to the lion in Daniel's den. And then, during the sermon, you urged the congregation to follow in the lootsteps of the ford. But perhaps you were widest of the mark during the reading of the announcements. I'm afraid there isn't going to be a peter-pull at St. Taffy's."

(599)

Finding her husband in bed with a long-haired lovely, the wife furiously picked up an ashtray, ready to launch it at him. "She's just a poor hitchhiker I picked up on the highway," the man tried to explain. "She was hungry, so I brought her home and fed her. Then I saw her sandals were worn out, so I gave her that old pair you haven't worn in at least twelve years. Then I noticed her shirt was torn, so I gave her an old blouse you haven't looked at since 1969. And her jeans were all patched, so I gave her an old pair of slacks you never wear. But as she was leaving, she asked me, "is there anything else your wife doesn't use?"

(600)

ADVICE TO BRIDES

If you don't want your marriage
To end in divorce,
Forget that your first love
Was hung like a horse!

(601)

Some Indian braves out hunting came upon a sleeping gorilla, which had escaped from a circus. Not knowing what it was, they ran and got the chief, a wise old man who had seen seventy summers. He looked it over and announced sagely, "Many moons ago on this spot, I screwed a bear. Do you think that thing could be my son?"

(602)

1 greased my hand and pulled it out soft,
I squeezed it as though to make it cough.
I rubbed it with my hands to make it slick,
I stretched it out so it wasn't so thick.
I felt it harden in my hand ...
The feeling then was simply grand!
It grew and hardened more and more;
I used both hands to keep it off the floor.
I'm not bragging ... both hands are handy
When pulling taffy to make some candy.
Would you like to have a piece?

(603)

OLD SONG - NEW LYRICS
"I WANT A TOOL"
I want a tool, just like the tool
That hung on Dear Old Dad.
It was a tool, and the only tool
that Mother ever had.
A real big, swinging tool, That built up fast,
It pumped like thunder
And would last and last ...
I want a tool, just like the tool
That hung on Dear Old Dad!

(604)

When the town fire siren sounded, a man at the bar put down his drink and started to run out. The man standing beside him remarked, "I didn't know you were a volunteer fireman." He answered, "I'm not...but my girlfriend's husband is!"

(605)

BUMPER STICKER

"This car is driven by sex instructor - First Lesson Free!

(606)

The college girl was going back to school on the train, with her lunch packed in a zipper bag by her mother. She put the bag on the seat beside her and fell asleep. A young man pushed her zipper bag over, sat down beside her and fell asleep too. While the girl was asleep, she dreamed she was so hungry she reached over and unzipped her lunch bag and began eating her lunch. "Oh, goody!" she cried in her sleep. "Two hard boiled eggs and the neck of the chicken!"

(607)

Little Helen was playing in the yard and she hollered in the house, "Momma, there's a soldier coming up the sidewalk." Her mother yelled, "You get in this house until he passes." Susie screamed, "There's a sailor with him." The mother hollered, "Bring your brother inside, too! " Susie yelled, "There's a marine, too." Mother shrieked, "Don't just stand there... hide the dog!"

(608)

A young member of the K K K was in the maternity ward waiting room for several hours. When the doctor came in Bill asked nervously, "Did she have anything yet?" Doc said, "Yes, she had three healthy boys." Bill boasted, "I'm not surprised it was more than one... I've got a cock like a stove pipe." The doctor grunted, "Well you' better blow the soot out of it. They're all three black!"

(609)

After a wild freeway chase, the motorcycle cop waved the speeding sports car over to the curb. When he walked up to the driver's window, he was surprised to find a very attractive redhead behind the wheel. "Ma'am," he said, "I'm afraid we're going to have to give you a breathalyzer test to see whether or not you've been drinking. The test was taken and as the officer eyed the results, he said, "Lady, you've had a couple of stiff ones." "That's amazing!" the girl cried. "You mean it shows that, too?"

(610)

An old man was polishing the antique lamp he'd just purchased in a junk shop, when a genie popped out of a cloud of smoke and granted him three wishes. The lucky lamp owner immediately asked for a new car and $10,000,000, whereupon a shiny Cadillac filled with starts of $1000 bills appeared. With His eyes gleaming, the elderly fellow used his last wish. "I want to be between the legs of a beautiful woman." The genie vanished back into the lamp and the old gentleman turned into a kotex!

(611)

The not-too-bright husband arrived home to find his wife in bed with a man. In a mad rage, he opened a dresser drawer, took out a loaded pistol and pointed it at his own head. "Are you crazy?" Yelled the lovers from the bed. "Just wait!" the husband said triumphantly. "You two are next!"

(612)

The parents of a popular high school girl were reading in bed one night when the mother looked at the father and said, "What do you think, Harry? It's past one o'clock. Shouldn't I go downstairs and tell Linda's boyfriend its time to go home?" Harry leaned over and pecked her on the cheek. "Now, now, dear," he chided smilingly, "don't you remember what it was like when we were courting?" The woman flung back the covers. "Harry," she screamed, "I'm going right down and throw that fucker out of the house!"

(613)

A golf pro manually guiding a shapely pupil through her swing somehow managed to entangle the back of her skirt in his trousers' zipper. Try as they might, they simply weren't able to separate the two garments, and the fellow and the girl were the object of amused looks from other golfers as they lock-stepped in some embarrassment toward the clubhouse for assistance. just as they arrived, a large dog came racing around a comer of the building and threw a bucket of water on them.

(614)

The kindergarten teacher held up the picture of an animal and asked,
What's this?'
"A horsy," one child answered.
"And this?" she asked.
"A piggy," replied another youngster.
"And now this one ?" asked the teacher, holding up the picture of a
deer. There was silence. "Come on, now children," she coaxed. "I'll
give you a hint. What does your mommy call your daddy when he's in
a loving mood? " I know, I know!" piped up a little girl, she calls
daddy "A horny bastard !"

(615)

Did you hear about the automobile mechanic who bought a hospital
and now he's making a fortune ? If you bring in your wife for surgery,
they give you a loaner.

(616)

Have you heard about the new two step method to cure yourself of
smoking in bed ? 1. Buy a water mattress. 2. Fill it with gasoline

(617)

Two boys went to their teacher the last day of school and asked if they
were promoted not. She told them that they had done real well, but
she had one more test for them. She wanted them to compose a four-
line poem and have the last line end in Tim Buck To. She said, "Tim
give yours first." He thought for a while and said, "As I traveled across
the sands, I lost my trusty caravan, with seas of green and sky's of
blue, I found it there in Tim Buck To. Then she said, "Johnny you
give yours" After thinking awhile he said, "Tim and I a went fishing
we saw three maidens in a tent, they were three and we were two, I
bucked one and Tim Bucked Two!

(618)

Talk about embarrassing moments, I went up to one woman and said, I'm so pleased to make your acquaintance. I've known your husband for ten years and I'm rather curious. Whatever happened to that dizzy blonde he used to be married to?" She said, "I dyed my hair."

(619)

I went up to one girl and said, "Gentlemen prefer blondes." She said, "I'm not really a blonde." I said, "Good. To tell you the truth, I am not really a gentleman!"

(620)

A man grew desperate at being dragged along by his wife on Saturday clothes buying expeditions to carry the packages and watch her purse. During one such excursion, she elbowed her way into the crowd at a lingerie sale counter, held up a pair of flimsy panties and asked her husband quite audibly if he liked them. "I certainly do, darling," he said brightly, "but I don't think your husband would approve of them at all! " The following Saturday, when his wife went shopping, he got to stay home and watch college football!

(621)

I wouldn't say he was dumb, but an 18-year-old told his girlfriend, after they parked on lovers' lane, "I wish you'd make up your mind, baby." "First you wanted me to get in the back seat of the car with you, and now you tell me to drive it home!"

(622)

While malting a delivery, the comparatively innocent grocery boy had fallen into the hands of a sexually aggressive woman. After he had undressed, as he was told to do, she said, "Let's do sixty-nine!" And before the lad had a chance to reply, she had done the positioning and begun. After it was over, she asked, "How was that? Did you like it?" "Great," the boy sighed, "but if you think I can do it sixty-eight more times, you're crazy!"

(623)

"Is there a woman here with an electric vibrator lodged in her? asked the chief of the emergency rescue squad. "Yes, it's my wife," replied the man who had opened the door. The paramedic frowned, "Those things are sometimes bitches to remove," he said. "Well, could you at least turn it off?" snapped the husband. It's fouling up the reception on my TV."

(624)

"It was a clear case of provocation, or even entrapment, your Honor," testified the man charged with indecent exposure. "Explain that statement," harrumphed the judge. "You see, this girl and I were drinking in a bar and got to talking, and compatibility in marriage came up and she asked, me, 'What do you want most in a woman?' "So, I showed her!"

A MAN HAS 17 PARTS THAT WON'T WORK!

10	Nails that won't nail.
2	tits that won't milk.
1	Belly button that won't button.
2	Balls that won't roll.
1	Cock that won't grow.
1	Ass that won't work.

What are you girls smiling for? You have a pussy that won't catch mice!

Ralph told Jeff, "I'm mad at you. I think you trained your dog to take bites out of my butt." Jeff reassured him, Rover's only a puppy. She's cutting teeth, so she nips at everything that sticks out." Ralph asked suspiciously, "Oh really.? Then how come she only attacks ME when I'm screwing your wife?

Some sophomore girls were talking in the hall, and I heard one say, "I get it every morning." Another bragged, "So do I... And in the evening too." A third girl admitted, "I'm not getting it from a regular boy, but I pick up one on the street most nights." "The fourth young lady confessed in a shy voice, "The man next door lets me have it... but sometimes his wife wants it first." Then with a very bored yawn, the fifth girl sighed and said, "I very seldom have time to read the newspaper!"

(628)

Said the judge to the starlet, "Now Liz, a divorce while you're pregnant? Gee whiz! She replied, looking sultry, "My grounds are adultery, why, even this child isn't his!'

(629)

TOASTING THE GROOM

"May your sorrows diminish,
May your fortunes increase
May you never give up
In the middle of a piece!"

(630)

Slow talking Slim finally dragged out the words to ask Ellie Sue to marry him. She didn't take long to answer yes. But two days before the wedding, the whole thing was called off. Slim's friends wanted to know why. He drawled. *"We was... sittin'... on the... porch,..... and I seen...Old Rover... scratchin'..... his back. I said....'After we're married... you'll do that..... To me." But..... by the time..... I finished ... and she turned to look..... old Rover was lickin....... his....... balls. "*

(631)

A woman confided to a psychiatrist, "I'm worried about my husband. He likes doggy sex." The doctor assured her, "That's not unusual. I enjoy doggy sex myself, and my wife doesn't find it abnormal." The woman retorted, "Well, I think it's weird...an so does our dog."

(632)

Want to guarantee our husband will take you out to eat?

A wise wife never tells her weary husband, "Let's go out and eat." She sighs, "Gosh, wouldn't it be relaxing to come home instead of going to a fancy restaurant, pull off all those uncomfortable dressy clothes, crawl into our nice soft bed, and gently screw ourselves to sleep? Have you given any thought to what you're going to order?

(633)

SIGN IN THE LOCAL "HOUSE OF PLEASURE"
Our prices are reasonable,
But we are not.
If you can't go three times,
You can sleep on a cot!

(634)

To tell the temperature in a room, count the strokes you give your sex partner in one minute and add 20. Then look at a thermometer. If it doesn't agree, you counted wrong or your timing is off. Keep on screwing until you get it right.

(635)

The doctor with the needle told little Helen, "Relax, it's only a little prick, You'll hardly even feel it." Little Helen just laughed and laughed, because she'd heard that line before ...

(636)

A woman had been married three times and never got sex. Her first husband was an oil well driller and spent all his time trying to decide where to sink his shaft. Her second was a packing clerk and couldn't figure out how to fold it to fit in the box. The third was a politician He came on strong, but once he got in, he didn't know what to do.

(637)

SENIOR CITIZEN POEM

When I was young and in my prime, I used to do it any time, but now I'm old, feeble and gray, and just wish I could do it once a day!

(638)

ANOTHER TOAST

Here's to you, so sweet and good,
God made you... I sure wish I could!

(639)

And then there was this electrician who traded his 40-year-old wife for two 20's. In about a week he discovered he wasn't wired for 220!

(640)

Homer called his girlfriend on the phone and said, "How about coming over and bringing me a *Sheep sandwich ?"* She said, "What's a Sheep sandwich?" Homer answered, "A little piece of ewe ..."

(641)

The man ran into the drug store and bought an entire gross (144) condoms. Later that same night, he returned to the drug store and started raising hell with the druggist, "Look you mother, you shorted me... there were only 143 rubbers in that carton you sold me!" The druggist reached down under the counter and came up with a single rubber. He handed it to the man and said, "I'm so sorry, it was my fault and I bet I spoiled your whole evening."

(642)

A lady visiting the local zoo tossed a monkey a peanut. He looked at it, stuck it up his rear and then ate it! The woman was embarrassed and called the zoo attendant to find out why the monkey would do such a disgusting thing. The zoo attendant informed her, "That's the smartest monkey we have in the zoo... Why, just last week (use a friend's name) came by and gave that monkey a fresh whole peach. It took over two weeks to get rid of the pit. From that day on .. If it don't fit, he don't eat it!"

(643)

One night after a revival meeting, the evangelist took a walk and happened to end up In the Red Light District of the city. At the next comer, he saw a hooker leaning against a light post. "I prayed for you last night," he said to the pretty girl. She smiled and said, "You didn't have to pray, you could of had me for I was home all evening!"

(644)

FRANK PRANK : Fellas, if you'd like to get one on your wife or lady friend, smuggle a large, warm weenie under the sheets. When the loving gets to grooving, stick the frankfurter between her legs so it stays in place. Then hop out of bed, exclaiming, "You go on without me ... I've got a phone call to make!" But NEVER try this trick when you're genuinely horny. chances aren't good that she'll let YOU replace the Hot Dog!

(645)

Have you heard about the new deodorant called "Gone?" . .. you spray it all over your body, you disappear... and everybody stands around and wonders where the smell is coming from !

(646)

The old man told his lawyer, "Make sure my Last Will and Testament states that my entire estate goes to my wife on the condition that she remarry within one month. I just want to be sure that there is at least one person in this world who is sorry I died!

(647)

1 wouldn't say Helen Patricia is dumb, but she works in a lawyer's office down town! This lawyer was planning a trip to Paris and gave Helen $100 with the instructions that she was to go out and bring back $ 100 worth of Francs! Helen Patricia was back in less than thirty minutes and brought back $ 100 sack full of hot dogs!

(648)

A girl went to see the doctor about the bad cuts and bruises on her elbows and knees. He asked her what happened and she shyly admitted that she got injured by having sex relations dog fashion. "The doctor asked her why she didn't do it like other girls... on her back She replied, "Doctor, did you ever smell a dog's breath?"

(649)

The egotistical moron was in the bar bragging to all who would listen, "You know, I have had sex with every woman in this town except my mother and my daughter!" The bartender leaned over the bar and whispered, "By golly, between the two of us, we have touched all the bases!"

(650)

Miss Debbie asked her fourth grade class to name some things that start with a "P." Little Johnny answered, " A day." She said, "No, Johnny, a day starts with a "D." Johnny just smiled and said, "Well, Miss Debbie, yours might .. But I always start my day with a good "P!".

(651)

 Did you hear about the guy who went to this fancy restaurant and ordered a steak? It smelled and it tasted rotten and you couldn't cut it with a chain saw. He called the waiter over and demanded a new, fresh steak. "There is absolutely nothing wrong with this meat," and to prove his point, the waiter picked up the steak and threw it out the front door where a passing dog gobbled it down. The dog then began to lick his butt. The customer looked at the waiter and said, "See? I told you it was rotten... look what that poor dog is doing to get the bad taste out of his mouth!"

(652)

ANOTHER TOAST!! Here's to the roses that are red, and the violets that are blue, if you are not going to screw me... then we are through!

(653)

Helen Patricia and her boyfriend were really quiet in the adjoining room, and Pop said to Mom, 'What do you reckon they might be doing right now?" Mom said, "Probably the same thing we did when we were their age" The old man yelled, "Let me at him... I'm going to kill that S.O.B.!"

(654)

Girls, have you seen the new bumper sticker? It reads:
"Firemen do it with bigger hoses!"

(655)

All the guys know this . . . "People who tie one on have a lot of trouble ripping one off."

(656)

We all have trouble with premature ejaculations once in a while, but they have come up with a sure fire way to prevent it. All you have to do is call your wife about an hour before you leave work and tell her to start without you!

(657)

And then there was the one about the father who was teaching his son to count! "Jimmy," asked his father, "What comes after ten?" Jimmy replied, "Well dad, Monday through Friday when you are working - it's the man next door!"

(658)

"Painless dentist my ass," laughed little Johnny. "He's no different from any other dentist I've been to!" "What do you mean," asked his mother. Johnny smiled, "He screamed like hell when I grabbed him by the balls!"

(659)

Did you hear the one about the little boy who brought home a terrible report card? His daddy looked at it and said, "I just don't understand how you could be so stupid! Both your Mom and Dad made decent grades in school. There will be no television for a month!" He then took the report card and signed it with a big "X." Johnny asked, " Why did you do that?" "Because son," his father replied, "I don't want your teacher to think that anyone with grades like yours has a father who can read and write!"

(660)

WHY I FIRED MY SECRETARY

I woke up early feeling a little depressed because it was my birthday and I thought, "Another year older," but decided to make the best of it. So I showered and shaved, knowing when I went down to breakfast my wife would greet me with a big kiss and say happy birthday, dear.

All smiles I went into breakfast and there sat my wife reading the newspaper as usual. She didn't say one word. So I got myself a cup of coffee and thought to myself, oh well, she just forgot. The kids will be in, in a few minutes all cheery and they will sing Happy Birthday and have a nice gift for me.

There I sat, enjoying my coffee, and I waited. Finally the kids came running in yelling "give me a slice of toast ... I'm late ... where's my coat? I'm going to miss the bus." Feeling more depressed than ever (continued on next page !)

I left for the office.

When I walked into the office, my secretary greeted me with a nice smile and a "Happy Birthday, Boss" and said, "I'll get you some coffee.' Her remembering made me feel a lot better.

Later in the morning my secretary knocked on my office door and said since it's your birthday why don't we have lunch together. Thinking it would make me feel better I said that's a good idea.

So we locked up the office and since it was my birthday I said why don't we drive out of town and have lunch in the country instead of going to the usual place. So we drove out of town and went to a little out-of-the-way place and had a couple of martinis and a nice lunch, and started driving back to town when my secretary said why don't we go by my place and I will fix you another martini.

It sounded like a good idea since we didn't have anything to do in the office anyway. So we went to her apartment and she fixed us both a martini and after a while she said if you will excuse me I think I will slip into something more comfortable and she left the room. In six minutes she opened her bedroom door and came out carrying a big birthday cake and following her was my wife and all my kids and there I sat with nothing on but my socks!

(661)

JUST A LINE!

Just a line to say I'm living - that I'm not among the dead; though I'm getting more forgetful and mixed up in the head.

For sometimes I can't remember when I'm standing by the stair, if I must go up for something or I've just come down from there.

And before the frig, so often, my poor mind is filled with doubt - have I just put the food away, or have I come to take some out?

And there's times when it is dark, with my night cap on my head, I don't know if I'm retiring or just getting out of bed.

So if it's my turn to write you, there's no need in getting sore, I may think I have written and don't want to be a bore.

So remember, I do LOVE YOU, and I wish that you were near, but now it's nearly mail time, so I must say "Goodbye, dear."

There I stood beside the mailbox with a face so very red, instead of mailing you my letter, I had opened it instead!

Warm wishes to all of you, from all of us.

(Author Unknown)

(662)

Just a thought - - - "I married her because we have so many faults in common.

(663)

MARITAL BLISS...

Mrs.: Do you still love me?

Mr.: Yes, but I would enjoy it more if you moved a little bit!

CAUTION TRAVELERS
The 747 Has Everything!

A man traveling by plane was in urgent need of using the Men's room. Each time he tried the door it was occupied. The stewardess, aware of his predicament, suggested that he use the Ladies room, but cautioned him against pressing the buttons on the wall. The buttons were marked WW, WA, PP, and ATR. Eventually his curiosity got the better of him and sitting there he carefully pressed the first button marked WW. Immediately, the warm water sprayed gently over his entire ass. He though, "Golly, these gals really have it made." Not yet satisfied, he pressed the next button marked WA. Warm Air dried his ass completely. This he thought was out of this world. The button marked PP, when pressed, yielded a large powder puff, which patted his bottom lightly with a scented perfume powder. Now, he thought . . . for the last button. Time passed and he was aware of nothing more until he awoke in the hospital In a panic, he buzzed for the nurse. When she appeared he cried out, "What happened? The last thing I remember was being in the Ladies' room, aboard a plane." The nurse replied, "so you were, but you were cautioned about pressing any button on the wall. You were doing great until you pressed the button marked ATR, which stands for AUTOMATIC TAMPAX REMOVER. Your penis is under your pillow.

COME FLY WITH ME !

CHAIN LETTER FOR WOMEN ONLY

This letter was started by a woman like yourself in the hopes of brining relief to other tired and discontented women.

Unlike most chain letters, this one does not cost anything. Just send a copy of this letter to five of your friends who are equally frustrated. Then, bundle up your husband or boyfriend, and send him to the woman whose name appears at the top of this list, and add your name to the bottom of the list.

When your name comes to the top of the list, you will receive 16,877 men ... one of them is bound to be a lot better than the one you already have.

Do not break the chain. One woman broke the chain and got her own son-of-a-bitch back. At this writing, a friend of mine already received 184 men. They buried her yesterday, but it took three undertakers 86 hours to get the smile off her face, and two days to get her legs together so they could close the coffin.

Hurry up and send this along, so my name can move up faster.

A couple, aged 67, went to the doctor's office. The doctor asked "What can I do for you?" The man said, "Will you watch us have sexual intercourse?" The doctor looked puzzled, but agreed. When the couple had finished, the doctor said, 'There is nothing wrong with the way you have intercourse." And he charged them $ 10.00. This happened several weeks in a row. The couple would make an appointment, go to have intercourse, pay the doctor and leave. Finally, the doctor asked, "Just exactly what are you trying to find out?" The old man said, "We're not trying to find out anything. She is married and we can't go to her house. I am married and we can't go to my house. Holiday Inn charges $52.00. Hilton Hotel charges $67.00. We do it here for $10.00 and I get back $8.00 from Medicare for a visit to the doctor's office."

DID YOU HEAR ABOUT JIMMY?

... One day Jimmy was bugging the hell out of his mom. Finally, she said, "Why don't you go across the street and watch the construction crew putting up that new building ... maybe you will learn something." Little Jimmy was gone for about two hours. When he got back, his mother asked him what he had learned. Jimmy replied, "First ... you put the goddamned door up, then the son-of-a-bitch doesn't fit. So, you have to take the cocksucker down. Then you have to take a cunt hair off of each side. Then you put the mother fucker back up. Jimmy's mother said......"You are going to have a talk with your dad when he comes home." When Jimmy's dad got home, Jimmy's mother said to Jimmy, "Tell your dad what you learned at the construction site today." Jimmy replied with the same answer that he had given his mom previously. His dad said "Jimmy, go get a switch." Jimmy replied, "Fuck you ... that's an electrician's job!"

The newly-married Italian couple came home to Brooklyn from their honeymoon and moved into the upstairs apartment they'd rented from the groom's parents. That night, the father of the groom was awakened from his deep sleep by his wife nudging him by hitting his stomach with her elbow. "Tony, listen!" she whispered. He listened. Upstairs, the bed was creaking in rhythm. The wife said, "Come on, Tony!" So Tony rolled on top of her and screwed. He was trying to fall back to sleep when, fifteen minutes later, the same sounds were heard. The wife said, "Tony! Listen to them! Come on, Tony!" Once again, Tony got on top of her and had sex. A short time later, the bedsprings upstairs began to squeak again. And again the wife nudged her husband. "Tony, listen! " At this, Tony leaped from the bed, grabbed a broom, and banged the handle against the ceiling as he shouted, "Hey, kids, cut it out! You're killing your old man!"

THE TALE OF THE BC.

My friend is a rather old fashioned lady, always quiet, delicate and very elegant, especially in the language she uses. She and her husband were planning a weeks vacation in Florida, so she wrote to a particular campground and requested a reservation. She wanted to make sure the campground was fully equipped, but really didn't know how to ask about the toilet facilities. After much deliberation, she finally came up with the old-fashioned term "BATHROOM COMMODE." But when she wrote that down, she still thought that she might be being too forward. So she started the letter all over again and this time referred to the "Bathroom Commode" merely as the "B.C." What she wrote was . . . "Does the campground have its own B.C.?"

Well, the campground owner wasn't old fashioned at all, and when he got the letter, he just couldn't figure out what the woman was talking about. That "B.C." business really stumped him" After worrying about it for a while, he showed the letter to some of his regular campers, but they too could not figure out what the lady meant when she referred to the "B.C.." So, the campground owner finally came up with the idea that the term B.C. must mean that the lady wanted to know the location of the, local BAPTIST CHURCH. He immediately sat down and wrote the following reply ...

Dear Madam:

Please forgive my delayed reply to your most welcome letter. I now take pleasure in informing you that the "B.C " is located 9 miles north of the campground and is capable of seating 350 people at one time. I do admit it is quite a distance away if you are in the habit of going regularly, but no doubt you will he pleased to know that a great number of people take their lunches along and make a day of it. They usually arrive early and stay late.

The last time my wife and I went was six years ago, and it was so crowded that we had to stand up the whole time we were there. It

(continued on next page)

continued ....

may, interest you to know that right now there is a Church Supper planned to raise money to purchase more seats. They plan to hold the supper in the basement of the B. C . I am sorry to say that it pains me very much not to be able to go more regularly, but it surely is no lack of desire on my part. As we grow older, it seems to be more of an effort, particularly in cold weather.

If you decide to come down to our campground, perhaps I could go with you the first time you go, sit with you and introduce you to all the other folks from the area around this part of the country. You can be sure you will find this a very warm, friendly community.

Thanking you for your interest in our campground and we look forward to a personal meeting with you and your husband. It will be a pleasure to sit with you both and have a little chat.
Personally yours,
Ed Smith, Manager

(670)

They met in the lounge at the ski lodge, where poor snow conditions were always a subject of conversation. "The forecast mentions the possibility of three to five inches tomorrow, "sighed the cute coed, "but they went on to say there was no guarantee." "What they say and what it does are two different things" said the fellow softly, "but on the other hand, I can positively guarantee you seven inches tonight!"

(671)

Did you hear the one about the guy who was dissatisfied with his penis transplant operation? His hand rejected it!

(672)

The company is going to freeze my wages
and a tear forms in my eye
Elephants work for peanuts,
and, now so do I !

(673)

Did you hear about the campground that was raided because they had a six-pack ? Three couples in one sleeping bag!

(674)

"I'm not scoring much these days and I think I know why !" My girlfriend calls me "Don Juan," which I assume means, "after Juan, I am Don."

(675)

Remember the story about the lady who got on the bus with three sets of twins? The bus driver looked her up and down and asked, "My God lady, do you always have twins?" to which the lady replied, "Oh no, thousands of times, we don't get anything."

(676)

The fraternity president asked the cute little coed, "How many beers does it take to make you dizzy?" "Four or five" she replied, "and don't you call me dizzy!"

(677)

Did you hear about the 80-year-old man who was accused of "Rape," but was later acquitted because the evidence would not stand up in court?

(678)

Don't forget the story about the drunk walking home about 6:00 A.M. when he noticed a man on a front yard doing pushups. The drunk watched him for a few moments and then went over and tapped him on the shoulder, "Pardon me sir, I don't want to bother you, but I've got to tell you, your girl must have gone home a long time ago. !"

(679)

The young man met his ex-wife at a party and after about 5 or 6 drinks, he invited his ex to go to his apartment for sex. "Over my dead body," she replied. Her former husband downed his drink and said, "Well, I see you haven't changed a bit!"

(680)

Every Saturday night Ike, the ranch hand, rode into town and got drunk in the saloon. One night his friends played a trick on him... they turned his saddle around on his horse with the horn facing the rear. The next morning he was complaining, "I sure had a tough time getting home last night. Some S.O.B. cut off my horse's head, and I had to guide him all the way home with my finger sticking in his wind pipe!"

(681)

Two men sitting in a bar noticed a fellow wearing a peculiar suit, with lace on the lapels, sleeves and trouser cuffs. Overcome, one of the men went over and said, "Look fella, just why in the hell are you wearing a lacy suit like that?" The fellow replied, "It's like this... I told my wife to go down to Sears and get me a seersucker suit, and by mistake she went to Cox's Department Store and came home with a damn cocksucker suit!"

(682)

A man sat In the bar for twelve straight hours, drinking one beer after another, and never once got up to go to the restroom. Then he stood up, walked out to the street and started to unzip. A passing cop said, "Hey friend, you can't do that here!" and the drunk replied, "Don't worry, I ain't.......I'm going to do *it way over yonder!"*

(683)

The traveling salesman, caught in a storm, was forced to spend the night at a farm house. They had only two beds, one for the farmer and his wife, one for Grandpa, so the salesman had to sleep with Grandpa. In the middle of the night Grandpa screamed out, "Bring on the girls! Bring on the girls," and woke up the salesman, who said, "Grandpa, I don't know what you have in mind, but what you have in your hand is *mine!"*

(684)

A lawyer calls his client to congratulate him on his twenty-fifth wedding anniversary. The guy greets him with total anger. "You son-of-a-bitch," he snarls over the phone. "The damn nerve you have to call me today of all days!" The lawyer is totally confused. "I don't understand," he mutters. "Twenty-five years ago, on my wedding night," the client explains, "I called you and told you I was gonna kill the bitch. You talked me out of it. You said they'd send me away for twenty five years." "Yes," remembers the lawyer. "Well," says the guy, "tonight I would have been a free man!"

(685)

IF YOU ARE THINKING ABOUT A DIVORCE
READ THIS...

Here's a word of advice.....if you want a good screwing from your wife, divorce her. I promise she'll give you one! My ex not only took the money and house, she turned my girlfriends against me. Even my own kids hate me now. And they're not even mine!

(686)

A husband frowned down at his wife and said, "How come the hair on your no-no is black ? It used to be blonde? " She smiled " Its still yellow, dearest, but you see, yesterday was payday at the coal mine."

(687)

Every marital argument has three sides...his side, her side, and "Well, I guess I'm sleeping on the couch again tonight!"

(688)

What's the difference between a prostitute, a housewife, and a Jewish American Princess in bed ? The prostitute says, "How do you want it?" The housewife says, "Could you please hurry it up?" and the Jewish American Princess says "Honey, don't you think the ceiling needs painting?"

(689)

Grandpa was lying on the couch, with the cat lying on his belly. Grandma was I knitting in the rocking chair, while their visiting grandson played on the floor. Suddenly, the old man tooted a real rip snorter. The cat jumped up, ran across the floor, and darted out through a hole in the screen. The boy asked, "Grandpa, why did the kitty run away?" The old man said, "Well, son, Grandma's a little hard of hearing, and every time she smells a poop, she beats the hell out of the cat!"

(690)

Jimmy raised his hand in class. When Miss Babbitt opened her mouth to answer, some joker let fly with a spitty paper wad and caught her right between the teeth. She spluttered, "That does it! I'M GONNA FLUNK THE NEXT PERSON WHO SHOOTS OFF A WAD! "Now, Jimmy, what do you want?" He blushed, 'I want to go to the boys room, but after what you just said... forget it!"

(691)

The Russian army places an order with an American company for twenty million condoms sixteen inches long and four inches in diameter. The president of the company consults with Secretary of Defense Weinberger to see if its okay to do business with the 'Evil empire.' Cap gives his approval, but specifies that each box of condoms must be stamped "small."

(692)

My secretary showed up with a black eye last Monday, and everybody asked her how it happened. She said shyly, "My husband did it to me." A couple of other girls gasped at the same time, "But we thought he was out of town!" The battered bride murmured, "So did I!"

(693)

Willie walked into a tavern and said, "Give me a double shot of bourbon, and did you hear the one about the President?" The bartender snarled, "WE don't talk politics here." Willie smiled, "That's okay with me. Did you hear about the Pope?" The bartender spat out, "We don't talk religion here, either." Willie downed his drink and asked, "Is it okay to talk about sex?" The bartender agreed, "Now that would be all right." Willie said, "OK Buddy, fuck you!"

(694)

Trucker Tom picked up two girl hitch hikers. As they were trucking along, he ogled their goodies and said, "I wonder what my wife will say when I pull into town with two pregnant women." One of the girls exclaimed, "Do you think we look pregnant?" Tom admitted, "Not in the least baby, but we still have a long way to go."

(695)

Did you ever stop to think that the difference between making love to a girl and making love to a woman can be as much as 20 years in some states?

(696)

Did you hear about the Indian who walked up to this cute little coed and said: "Honey, would you like to take a chance on this Indian blanket ?"

(697)

Two young nuns were returning from church one night when they were confronted by two hoodlums. "Dear Lord," prayed one of the nuns, "forgive them for they know not what they are doing." The other nun replied, "Not so loud Sister, this one does."

(698)

Then there was the one about the drunk who walked up behind the mounted Policeman in New York, put his finger in the back end of the horse. The cop looked around and said, " What in the hell are you doing?" The drunk said, "Well, I have a fever blister on my lips and I take this finger out of the horse and wipe it on my lips." The cop shook his head and replied, "You dumb ass, that's not going to cure your fever blister." "I know that," said the drunk, "but it sure as hell will keep me from licking my lips! "

(699)

How about Mrs. Jones who bought herself a bicycle and proceeded to peddle her ass all over town!

(700)

The young college physician was at a loss to understand why so many coeds were visiting his office for pregnancy tests. "There seems to be something in the air this time of year that causes young girls to get pregnant" he mentioned to an older colleague. "What is it, I wonder?' "Their legs," replied his friend.

(701)

Have you heard about a pair of hippie parents who had their babies christened in Greenwich Village so the little one could have a fairy godfather?"

(702)

A middle-aged housewife was bragging to her husband about her still slim figure. "I can still get into the same skirts that I had before we were married," she said. Without glancing up from his newspaper, her husband replied, "I wish to hell I could."

(703)

Then there were the two gay judges who tried each other!

(704)

Rushing into the frontier saloon, the Revival Evangelist yelled ... "Repent, you sinners" "Drinking that horrible fluid will send you all to hell. Join with me ... all of you who want to go to heaven, stand up here with me." All but one drunk staggered up on the platform. The preacher looked down and shouted....."Don't you want to go to heaven?" "No, I don't," replied the drunk. "You mean to tell me that you don't want to go to heaven when you die?" Asked the Minister. "Oh sure," replied the drunk, when I die. I thought you were making up a load right now."

(705)

And then, there was this 80-year-old lady who went to her doctor to tell him she needed some help. The doctor said, "Now, just what is your problem?" "I am losing my desire for sex" the lady replied. The doctor was flabbergasted and aside, "Come on now, just when did you find out you were losing your desire for sex?" She said, "Last night and then again this morning!"

(706)

How about the little old lady that, went to the Police Station and told the cop she had been raped. "The Policeman asked her, "Lady, how old are you?" She said she was 82. "And when were you raped?", replied the Officer. She said, "It was November 8, 1947." The Policeman shook his head and asked "If this happened so many years ago, why are you reporting it now?" The little old lady replied, "I'm not reporting, I just want to talk about it."

(707)

The young wife was in the bathroom toweling off after the morning shower when she heard the back door slam. Thinking it was her husband, she called out, "I'm here darling, I've been waiting for you." All of a sudden a deep voice replied, "Ma'am, I think you ought to know, I'm not your regular milkman !"

(708)

Two drunks were sitting at the bar talking about their home lives.....One said "Since we moved across town, our night life has improved 100 percent!" The other drunk say's "What have they got over there that they don't have here?" "Well, we have this little tavern only a block from home and they have this contest every Saturday night; all the stools and seats are numbered and when they draw a number and you have that number, you get to go upstairs for one whole hour of really good sex !" "You're kidding!", said his friend, "Did you ever win?" The first drunk, said, "No, not me personally, but my wife has won three Saturday nights in a row!"

(709)

After a heart transplant operation, the patient was receiving instructions from his doctor. He was placed on a strict diet, denied tobacco and advised to get at least 8 hours sleep each night. Finally, the patient asked, "What about my sex life, doc? Will it be all right for me to have intercourse?" "Just with your wife," replied the doctor. "We don't want you to get too excited! "

(710)

Most major cities have a "Dial-a-Prayer" number for anyone requiring religious reassurance in the form of a brief, prerecorded sermon. Now there's talk of establishing a similar number for all the atheists. When you dial it, no one answers.

(711)

Do you know why Democrats have more children than Republicans? After all, whoever heard of anyone enjoying a good piece of elephant?

(712)

One summer night, as the elderly couple sat on the front porch looking at the cemetery across the street, the woman remarked, "You know, dear, every time I think of our wonderful daughter lying over there, it makes me want to cry. "I know," the man agreed, "it saddens me too. Sometimes I even wish she were dead."

(713)

Wishing to surprise her husband with a new wig she had just bought, the wife put it on and strolled unannounced into her husband's office. "Do you think you could find a place in your life for a woman like me ?" she asked sexily. "Not a chance," he replied. "you remind me too much of my wife !"

(714)

After 18 holes of golf, two men were changing their clothes in the country club locker room. One of the men started putting on a girdle and the other, quite astonished, said "Since when did you start wearing that thing?". Shaking his head resignedly, the first man replied, 'Ever since my wife found it in the glove compartment of our car! ."

(715)

MEN .. What are two words you don't want to hear when you are standing at a urinal? "NICE DICK!"

(716)

What did Jeffrey Dalhmer say to Lorena Bobbitt? "You gonna eat that?"

(717)

Did you hear about the sweet, innocent looking young lady who told the judge she had been raped? When the judge asked the rapist if he had anything to say before he pronounced him guilty the stud stood up and said, "Well Judge, at least I had the decency to do it to her with her panties on." The young girl jumped and shouted angrily, "No, you didn't... you know damn well that I took them off before you started!" The judge said, "Case Dismissed!"

(718)

The next time someone gives you the "finger," you ask them, "What's that... is it your age, your IQ or is the number of parents listed on your birth certificate?"

(719)

Remember the comedian who was on stage trying to entertain when a man in the front row kept interrupting him with a really loud cough. The comedian let it go for a little awhile and when the man got louder, he said, "Hey Buddy, you want a cure for that cough?" "All you have to do is drink a full bottle of Milk of Magnesia." "Tomorrow morning when you get up, you'll be afraid to cough!"

(720)

CONFUCIUS SAYS: Better to sleep with old hen than pullet!

(721)

Have you noticed how many couples are naming their first girl baby "April" ? It's a private joke to remind them of the "noon quickie" they enjoyed on April One when they were fooling around!

(722)

Have you heard about the High School cheer leaders who were expelled from school? At a basketball game they composed their own cheer that went like this ...."PORK CHOPS, GREEN BEANS, MASHED POTATOES, GRAVY... LET'S GET TOGETHER AND MAKE A LITTLE BABY!"

(723)

The young drunk was seated beside the old drunk at the local bar when the youngster says, "Hey Pop, do you know the most useless thing on a woman?" The old drink replied, "No, what?" The young drunk says, "Oh, a man about your age!"

(724)

The sheriff was driving along and noticed this drunk throwing bowling balls off the over-pass. He pulled up close and said, "Hey Buddy, what the hell are you doing?" The drunk replied, "It's a big secret...I figure if we destroy all their eggs there won't be nobody but us white people on earth!"

(725)

Two friends were drinking when suddenly one of the men exclaimed, "Wow, look at that pair of boobs that just bounced in! I wonder if she'd let me have a little?" The other guy replied, "I really don't know whether she will or whether she won't but, if she does, I would sure appreciate you telling me... I'm her husband! "

(726)

A drunk, asked a guy standing beside him at the local bar, "Did you spill a glass of beer on me?" The fellow said, no, so he asked the man on the other "Hey Buddy, did you spill beer on me?" The other guy answered, "No, I didn't." The drunk looks down at his pants and sighs, "Just as I thought, I'm peeing my pants!"

(727)

The man bought a pet monkey and brought it home to his wife. She said, "What is it going to eat?" and hubby replied, "Just what we do, dear." Then she asked, "Where is the monkey going to sleep?" And he answered, "Right in bed with us, dear." So she said, "But what about the smell?" And hubby said, "Well, I got used to the smell, so I guess the monkey can too!"

(728)

The newlyweds stopped at a farm house and made a deal to bed down for the night. By noon the next day they were not up yet so the farmer hollered for them to come get some breakfast. "We're living on the fruits of love," called the groom. "Go ahead and eat your fruit," hollered the farmer, "but quit throwing the damned rubbers out the window . . . they're choking the ducks!"

(729)

The maniac in Ward B of the Coo coo Hospital was explaining why he was there. "One time I was washing dishes and broke one, so my wife said, "Why don't you just break 'em all?" So I did. Another time I was washing the windows and broke one, so my wife said, 'Why don't you just break 'em all?" so I did. Then one night in bed I made a pass at her and she said, "'Cut it out!" ... And say fellow," said the maniac, extending a cupped hand, "Have you ever seen one of these CLOSE UP?"

(730)

Homer and Jed had a thriving business and a private airplane. They also went off on escapades. On this particular trip with two beautiful blondes, Homer, who was piloting, called on the intercom, and whispered, "Quick, the plane's afire! Get your parachute, we gotta to jump!" Jed Said, "What about the girls?" Said Homer, "Screw the girls!" Said Jed, "You think we got time?"

(731)

Did you hear about the drunk who put a nickel in the parking meter? He stood back for a second and said, "My God! I've lost 60 pounds!"

(732)

The bride and groom decided to take Amtrak from New York to Los Angeles for their honeymoon. When they arrived at the train station, they were informed that all sleepers were sold out with the exception of one upper berth. After talking it over, the newly married couple decided that they had no choice, so they purchased the tickets. Once aboard the train, the groom told his bride, "Honey, since we are going to be in such close quarters, and since I packed us a little lunch, every time you want to have sex, you simply say "Honey, would you like an orange ?" I'll know what you mean and we won't be embarrassed because the other passengers hear us. Their plan worked remarkably and every hundred miles either the bride or the groom would ask, "Dearest, would you like to have another orange?" About 50 miles before they reached LA, the groom once more said, "Honey, we are almost there ... would you like another orange before we get off the train?" With that, the passenger in the bunk below couldn't take it any more and yelled at the top of his voice, "Hey kids, why don't you try an apple, I'm getting orange juice all over me!"

(733)

You know, the trouble with being a best man in a wedding is the fact that you don't have the opportunity to prove it!

(734)

There was a fellow who was determined that the gal he'd marry had to be an innocent virgin. After much thought, he devised a clever way to test his dates to see if they were virgins ... he'd open his fly, pull out his unit and ask them what it was. Surely any girl who didn't know what it was would have to be a virgin. He traveled far and wide, tried his test on many, many girls, but always they knew the answer to his question. Finally, after several years, he was about to lose his faith in womanhood, when he met an innocent-looking young girl way back in the hills of Kentucky. When he popped his manhood out and popped the question to her, she smiled and said, "Oh, I dunno, I'd say it's a toy !" Well, the search was ended, and they were soon married. The first night of the honeymoon, he undressed and said, Helen Patricia, you were wrong in thinking this thing here is a toy, and tonight I'm going to show you what it really is!" She smiled and said, "Golly, I'd still say it's a toy." A bit impatient, he insisted, "No, Helen Patricia, it's really a man's screwing machine." She replied, "Well, it looks more like a toy to me. If you call that thing a screwing machine, you ought to see the one on my cousin Homer!"

(735)

A guy comes home early and catches his wife in bed with the doctor. "What the hell are you doin, Doc ?" "I'm taking your wife's temperature, that's what I'm doing." The guy goes to the closet and gets his shotgun. "Well, that thing better have numbers on it when you pull it out!"

What do a woman's breasts and toy train sets have in common ?
They're both meant for children, but Daddies love playing with them
too!

Then there was this lumberjack who went to the whore house and told
the madam that he wanted something a little different and special
tonight. The Madam thought for a moment and came up with one of
her special girls who called herself "Hurricane Gussie." The
lumberjack said, "OK, sounds good to me" and then proceeded to go
upstairs, get his clothes off and was laying on the bed when this big
buxom of a woman came in the room with her cheeks all puffed up
and blowing time after time. The lumberjack asked, "What the hell are
you doing?" She said, "Well, I am Hurricane Gussie and those are the
warm tropical breezes that come with the hurricane." Then she jumped
up on the bed, straddled the lumberjack and started hitting him in the
head with her giant titties. Again, he was baffled and asked, "Now,
what are you doing?" She said, "Well honey, I'm Hurricane Gussie,
and those are the coconuts falling from the trees hitting you in the
head." He said, "Well, it's got to get better than this before I start liking
it." Just then Hurricane Gussi stood up on the bed and started peeing
all over the lumberjack's stomach. "My God," said the lumberjack, as
he started squirming to get out of the bed, "what are you doing now?"
"Those are the warm tropical rains that come with the Hurricane!" The
lumberjack, finally was able to get out of bed and started getting on his
pants when Hurricane Gussie said, "You're not leaving are you
honey?" The lumberjack, replied, "Hell yes, I'm leaving. Who can
screw in weather like this?"

Did you hear about the girl who gave her boyfriend a birthday present?
Now, he is giving her a Mother's Day present!

THE CONTRACTOR OF THE FAMOUS SEARS TOWER IN CHICAGO TELLS THIS STORY... These workers were on the 20th floor of the unfinished building when one of them asked his supervisor if he could go down and use the bathroom. The supervisor informed him that he was working by the hour and it would be too costly to allow him to go all the way down to the street. The supervisor said, "I have a better idea... why don't you take this 2 inch by 12 foot long board, place it so it protrudes out 4 or 5-foot over the street below. I will stand on this end while you walk out and relieve yourself."

The supervisor stood on his end of the board and the worker walked out to where he was directly over the street. Just then the phone rang on the 20th floor and the supervisor, forgetting what he was doing, stepped off the board to answer the phone.

The next morning there was an autopsy at the building site and the Coroner asked all the workers if they knew why this accident happened. NO one answered the question for about two minutes, and then one of the workers spoke up and said, "I really don't know what happened, but I think it had something to do with sex."

The Coroner asked "Why do you say that ?" "Well..."the worker said, "I was working on the 5th floor when the guy came down - he was holding his dick with one hand and was waving the other in the air as he yelled "Where did that cocksucker go ?"

This young couple enjoyed a wonderful honeymoon at one of the great motels on Miami Beach. When they checked out with the desk clerk the groom asked exactly how much do we owe for the great accommodations? The desk clerk replied, "Your total bill is only $200 a piece." The groom wrote a check for $ 1,000 and walked out the front door with his bride.

(741)

Then there was the one about the preacher who had this talking parrot. Every time he would bring a girl home with him, the parrot would meet them at the front door and say, "You're gonna get screwed ... you're gonna get screwed." This went on for over a year and the preacher had had it! He told the parrot, "The next time I bring a girl home and you *say you're gonna get screwed,* I'm going to cut your throat and flush you down the toilet. Sure enough, that very night the preacher invited another girl to come over for dinner and as usual, the parrot said the same thing. The preacher grabbed a butcher knife and proceeded to cut the parrot's throat and toss him in the toilet. After a wonderful dinner, the girl excused herself and headed for the bathroom. He rushed in and found the parrot floundering around in the water, very much alive. The preacher said, "You S.O.B., I cut your throat and I thought you were dead! " The parrot looked up and replied "Hell no, you didn't kill me. If that girl can live with a gash like that, I can sure live with a little cut like this!"

(742)

Have you heard the one about the Policeman who found a drunk standing out in the street? The drunk asked the Policeman to help him. He told the cop, "Somebody stole my car and it was right here at the end of this little ignition key" The Officer said, "OK, let's go down to the station and report it... but, before we go, would you please zip up your pants!" The drunk looked down, noticed the open fly and said, "My God! Somebody stole my girlfriend too!"

(743)

HERE IS A CUTE TOAST FOR YOUR NEXT NEIGHBORHOOD PARTY
Martini's at parties are deceiving...
Take two at the very most
Take three and you are under the table...
Take four and you are under the host!

(744)

Doughtery came home late one night a trifle "under the weather."
Since he couldn't find the key to the front door he began climbing
through the window. He was almost inside when a policeman stopped
him. "Sure this is my house!" Dougherty blubbered, pulling the cop in
after him. "This is my hall, that's my carpet, this is my bedroom, that's
my bed, that's my wife, and you see that guy in bed with her? That's
me!"

(745)

Adam and Rodney Williams were twins, Adam was married.
Rodney owned a dilapidated rowboat. Strangely enough, on the day
that Adam's wife died, Rodney's rowboat sank.

The next day, Aunt Marjorie mistook Rodney for the brother
whose wife had just died. "Oh, Mr. Williams," she said kindly, "I'm so
sorry to hear of your loss!" "I'm not a bit sorry for she was a rotten old
thing from the start," said Rodney. "Her bottom was all chewed up,
she smelled of fish, and the first time I used her, she made water faster
than anything I ever saw. It finally got so I couldn't handle her."

"Then one day, some guy used her and she leaked like the dickens.
But the thing that finished her was one day I rented her to some guys
looking for a good time. I explained to them what she was like, but
they said they'd take a chance with her anyway. Well, the damn fools
tried to use her all at one time and that was too much for her for she
cracked right up the middle. Aunt Marjorie fainted dead away.

(746)

A 16-year-old girl had been crossed in love, and decided to commit suicide. She purchased a mail order revolver, loaded it, and pressed the gun to her temple. But then she thought, "No, this would be messy and ruin my face. Mother would be furious. "So she lowered the gun to her heart and thought, "I might blow off my breasts. What an inglorious thing, to have to wear falsies to one's own funeral. " She placed the gun on her stomach, started to shoot, then muttered, "That catty Helen Aunt would say I did it to lose weight!" She moved the gun further, and stuck, it into her love channel. "This time I'm really going to do it," she declared and touched the trigger. But then she realized there would be abortion talk, and pulled it out again. A minute later, she said, "Never mind the scandal, I've got to die," and pushed the gun even deeper inside. Once again, she hesitated and pulled it out. Then she pushed it in ... pulled it out ... pushed it in ... pulled it out ... right now, you readers are probably wondering whether it ever went off. Well, you are right, it did, but the GUN didn't!

(747)

Old Pete Pawkin, the cattle rancher, had a strapping fine son, over 18, a real help with the cows. Pete decided his son should be married, so they saddled a pair of fine Pinto Ponies one day and rode to the Bar Six ranch, where the owner, Sam Starling, had the purtiest daughter you ever did see. Pete and Sam made a deal and the kids got married, then rode back home to the Pawkin layout, the Purty new bride riding behind her handsome husband. Early next morning, Pete's son came down with a long face, instead of his usual happy grin. "What's the matter, boy?" asked Pete. "Aw Paw," the kid answered, "She ain't got one of them things." Pete called the girl in, lifted up her skirt, and said, "What's THAT, then?" and the kid answered, "Well, I'll be darned! You know Pop, after the sheep, cows and pigs, I never knew girls, had it in front!"

(748)

"My wife is really bugging me," muttered the morose drinker to his bar companion. "It's nothing but, thanks for the five, Sam - if you can afford it!" or, "I've got to have six this time, Sam!" or, "Sam, couldn't you somehow manage to give me seven?" "What does she do with all that money?" asked his fellow drinker sympathetically. "Who's talking about money?" snapped Sam.

(749)

CIVIL SERVICE BLUES
I thought I'd be a G Girl and have a little fun
They took my application, and made me a GS- I
I wore a naughty little blouse that you could see right thru
My boss took one look at me, and made me a GS-2

I started some dictation with my skirt above my knees,
When I got through that letter, I became a GS-3

He gave my thigh a little pinch as he went out the door
I blinked my big blue eyes at him and got my GS-4

I felt so good one morning, it was good to be alive
I gave my fanny a wiggle, and soon a GS-5

My boss asked me to kiss him, and I showed him some new tricks
He must have liked the lesson, for he made me a GS-6

We went off for a weekend to his little seashore heaven
I guess I must have pleased him, cause I got my GS-7

My work must be improving, for I'm now a GS-8
But I don't know now if it's worth it cause, my God, I'm three weeks late!

(750)

The woman had been away for two days visiting a sick friend in another city. When she returned, her little boy greeted her by saying, "Mommy, guess what! Yesterday, I was playing in the closet in your bedroom and Daddy came into the room with the lady next door and they got undressed and got into your bed and then Daddy got on top of her . . . "

Sonny's mother held up her hand. "Not another word. Wait till your father comes home and then I want you to tell him exactly what you've just told me." The father came home. As he walked into the house, his wife said, "I'm leaving you. I'm packing now and I'm leaving you."

"But why . . . " asked the startled father. "Go ahead, Sonny. Tell Daddy just what you told me." . Well," Sonny said, "I was playing in your bedroom closet and Daddy came upstairs with the lady next door and they got undressed and got into bed and Daddy got on top of her and then they did just what you did with Uncle John when Daddy was away last summer."

(751)

A man who worked for the Fire Department came home from work one day and told his wife, "You know, we have a wonderful system at the job: at Bell 1 we all put on our coats; at Bell 2 we all slide down the pole, and when Bell 3 rings, we are on the truck and ready to go. From now on, we're going to run this house the same way. "When I say Bell 1," he said, "you strip naked." When I say Bell 2, you jump into bed, and at Bell 3, we're going to screw all night."

The next night, he came home from work and yelled, "Bell 1!" His wife immediately took off all her clothes. "Bell 2!" He hollered, and she jumped into bed. "Bell 3!" and he jumped on her and began to screw.

In a few minutes, his wife began to scream, "Bell 4" Bell 4" Stunned, her husband said, "What in the hell is Bell 4?" "More hose," she said. "You ain't no where near the fire!"

THE MAN WITH THE TWELVE BOTTLES OF WHISKY
IN THE CELLAR ...

I Had twelve bottles of whiskey in my cellar and my wife told me to empty the contents of each and every bottle down the sink "or else!"

So, I said I would, and proceeded with the unpleasant task. I withdrew the cork from the first bottle. I poured the contents down the sink, with the exception of one glass, which I drank.

I extracted the cork from the second bottle, and did like wise, with the exception of one glass, which I drank.

I then withdrew the cork from the third bottle and emptied the good old booze down the sink, except the glass which I devoured.

I pulled the cork from the fourth sink and poured the bottle down the glass, which I drank.

I pulled the bottle from the cork of the next, and drank one sink out of the next glass, and poured the cork down the bottle.

I poured the next cork from the throat, and pulled the sink down the bottle, and drank the glass. Then I corked the sink with the glass, bottled the drink, and drank the pour.

When I had everything emptied, I steadied the house with one hand and counted the bottles and corks and glasses with the other, which were twenty-nine. To be sure, I counted them again when they came by, and had seventy-five and as the house came by.

I counted them again, and finally I had all the houses and bottles and corks and glasses counted, except one house and one bottle, ,which I drank.

(753)

BIRTH OF A CANDY BAR

One Payday Mr. Goodbar wanted a Bit o'Honey, so he took Miss.Hershey behind the Power House on the corner of 5th Avenue and Clark. He took what he wanted feeling her Mounds and Almond Joy, which definitely made his Tootsie Roll. He let out several Snickers as he slipped his Butterfinger up her Kit-Cat at which of course, caused a Milky Way, she screamed O'Henry as she squeezed his Peter Paul and Zagnuts and told him he was better than 3 Musketeers. She soon became Chunky and 9 months later she gave birth to Baby Ruth.

(754)

THE CLINTON SPECIAL

PRESIDENT CLINTON, out traveling, was looking for a CALL GIRL and found three such ladies in a local lounge; a blonde, a BRUNETTE and a redhead. To the blonde he said, "I am the PRESIDENT OF THE UNITED STATES, and how much would it cost me to spend some time with you?" The shapely blonde replied, "for you, Mr. president, it will cost $500.00." To the brunette, he poised the same question, and she replied, "I will spend all the time you want for $ 1,000.00." When he approached the gorgeous redhead along similar lines, she replied, "if you can raise my skirt as high as my TAXES, get my pants down as low as my WAGES, and get that thing of yours as HARD AS TIMES ARE, and screw me as well as you do the PUBLIC, believe me, Mr. President, it won't cost you a damn cent!"

Jordan was young and he was horny. When he arrived at the Foreign Legion post he was disturbed by the total absence of females on the post. "Jeepers, creepers!" he said to the sergeant. "Don't you fellows have any sex here?" "Sure we do," said the sergeant. "It's just that we of the French Foreign Legion have to adapt to our environment." "I don't understand." "Well," the sergeant explained, "the camels come every Thursday afternoon at three o'clock." "Camels!" the young man snorted in disgust. "Huh!" But by Thursday, he couldn't wait. He stood at the edge of the camp scanning the horizon. At then to three, he could see a cloud of dust. It grew larger, and then a herd of about twenty camels came thundering into the camp. Jordon couldn't wait. Grabbing the first one by the bridle, he quickly began to fuck it. The sergeant ran up to him, "Private Jordon, what in hell are you doing?" "Christ, sergeant, it's easy enough to see!" "No, no, you fool! The camels come to take us to town so we can get the girls!"

(756)

On the final night of his first buying trip to Paris, a young furniture importer from America met an attractive French girl in the hotel elevator. She spoke no English, however, and neither could understand a word the other was saying until the resourceful merchant devised a means of communication for the occasion. Taking out a pencil and notebook, he drew a sketch of a taxi. She nodded approvingly, and off they went for a ride. A little later, he drew a picture of a table laden with food and wine bottles and when she nodded her consent, they headed for a sumptuous restaurant. After dinner, she was delighted with a sketch he made of a dancing couple, so they danced the evening away at a popular club. Finally the girl picked up the pencil and, with a knowing glance at her clever escort, she proceeded to make a crude drawing of what was clearly intended to be a four-poster bed. He stared at his charming companion in amazement; and he took her home, and kissed her good night on her doorstep. During the long ride back to his hotel, and even on his flight back home the following afternoon, he still couldn't figure out how she had known he was in the furniture business.

(757)

What do the words Hurricane, Tornado, Fire and Divorce have in common ? They describe four ways you can lose your house !

The circus was finishing its final performance in the country town when one of its zebras had a stroke. The local veterinarian prescribed a few weeks rest for the beast, so the circus owner made arrangements to board it at a nearby farm.

The zebra took to the new life immediately and spent the first day meeting all the animals of the barnyard.

He came across a chicken and said, "I'm a zebra, who are you?"

"I'm a chicken,'" said the chicken.

"What do you do?" asked the zebra.

"I scratch around and lay eggs," said the chicken.
Moving on, the zebra found a cow. He introduced himself saying, "I'm a zebra. Who are you?"

"I'm a cow," said the cow.

"What do you do?" asked the zebra.

"I graze in the field and give milk," said the cow.
The zebra met a bull next. "I'm a zebra," he said. "Who are you?"

"I'm a bull," said the bull.

"And what do you do?" asked the zebra.

"What do I do!" snorted the bull pawing at the turf with a forefoot.
"Why you silly looking ass ... you take off those damned stripped pajamas and I'll show you!"

I wouldn't say Homer was unlucky but he finally got married when...
his bride took off her make up; she was so ugly, Louie got a sex change operation so he wouldn't have to screw her. Then he found out she was gay

(760)

PLAYGIRL MAGAZINE
185 Fifty First Street, New York,, City, NY

Dear Mr.

We wish to thank you for your letter and pictures which we recently received from you. We regret to inform you that we will not be able to use your body in our next magazine centerfold.

On a scale from zero to ten, your body was rated "minus 2". The rating was done by a panel of women ranging in age from 65 to 85 years. We tried to have our panel of women in the 25 to 35 age bracket rate your body, but we couldn't get them to stop laughing long enough.

Should the taste of the American Women ever change so drastically that they would want YOU in the centerfold, you will be notified by this office. In the meantime, however, please don't call us, we'll call you.

Sympathetically,

Amanda Smith, Editor

Playgirl Magazine

(761)

While out walking on the African field one day, a missionary suddenly came face to face with a lion. Thinking that his situation was hopeless, he sank to his knees in prayer, but then became greatly relieved when the lion got down on its knees beside him. "Dear brother lion," said the missionary, "how heartening it is to find you joining me in Christian prayer when a few moments ago I feared for my life!"

"You really are a dummy" growled the lion, "Don't you realize I'm saying grace?"

I'M TIRED

Yes, I'm tired. For several years I've been blaming it on middle-age, iron poor blood, lack of vitamins, air pollution, water pollution, saccharin, obesity, dieting, underarm odor, yellow wax build up and a dozen other maladies that make you wonder if life is really worth living. But now I find out, taint that.

I'm tired because I'm overworked.

The population of this country is 200 million. 84 million are retired. That leaves 116 million to do the work. There are 75 million in school, which leaves 41 million to do the work. Of this total, there are 22 million employed by the government. That leaves 19 million to do the work. 4 million are in the armed forces, which leaves 15 million to do the work. Take from that total the 14,800,000 people who work for state and city government and that leaves 200,000 to do the work, There are 188,000 in hospitals, so that leaves 12,000 to do the work.

Now, there are 1 1,998 people in prisons, that leaves just two people to do the work. You and me. And, you're sitting there reading this. No wonder I'm tired!

Anonymous

NORTH POLE
NUMBER ONE CHRISTMAS TREE LANE
00076

My Dear Friend,

   Everyone gets dissatisfied with his job once in a while, but you haven't heard nothing until you have heard the woes of Santa Claus..... You think you got it bad....... ?

   All night long, soot in the chimneys, smelly socks, mean dogs, shot at, mistaken for a stork, driving all night in the damn snow, damn near got killed by a 747, Mrs. Claus was really pissed off because I got in so late and that isn't all.

   Donnor and Blitzen and Red-nosed Rudolph got the shits over Albuquerque and you should see my suit. The damn elves won't clean the sleigh unless I pay them double time. I am so sick of cookies and milk, I could vomit. The only highball I had all night is when I slipped getting into the damn sleigh. My prostrate is really giving me hell, pissed my pants at 80,000 feet and my pants froze to my seat.

   Allergic to pine needles, I itch all over. I think my hemorrhoids are back. How many times did you say, "Merry Christmas?" Merry Christmas, your ass. What the hell ... might as well wish you and yours a happy, prosperous New Year! You got to admit that whatever happens, it is going to be better than last year!

A CHAIN LETTER

Dear Friend:

This chain letter started with the hope of bringing relief and happiness to all tired husbands ... unlike most chain letters, this **does** not cost money. Simply send a copy of this letter to 6 of your married friends who are equally tired ... then bundle up your wife and send her to the man on the top of the list and add your name to the bottom of the list. When your name comes to the top of the list, you will receive 16,487 women and some of them will be dandies. Have faith in **the** letter ... one man broke the chain and got his old lady back.

Don't let this happen to you!

Sincerely,

A Good Friend,

PS: At the time of writing this, a friend of mine has received 365 women. They buried him yesterday and it took 7 Undertakers 36 hours to wipe the smile off his face.

(765)

NOW I LAY ME DOWN TO SLEEP

I PRAY MY PENIS I WILL KEEP

AND IF I WAKE AND IT IS GONE

I HOPE I FIND IT ON THE LAWN

I HOPE THE DOG THAT IS RUNNING FREE

DOESN'T SEE THAT LITTLE PART OF ME

MANY PRECAUTIONS I MUST TAKE

TO KEEP THIS PART I LOVE TO SHAKE!

MUCH ATTENTION I MUST PAY

TO ASSURE I PUT THE KNIVES AWAY

THE MOWER, CHAIN SAW, THE HATCHET TOO

WHY THERE'S JUST NO TELLING WHAT SHE'D DO

TO RID ME OF MY MANLY CHARM

I MUST KEEP IT SAFE, AWAY FROM HARM

SO I CROSS MY FINGERS, AS I CLOSE MY EYES

AND I CROSS MY LEGS TO AVOID SURPRISE!

(766)

THE STORY OF "MY MUDDER"

When my prayers were poorly said,

Who was it tucked me into bed,

And spanked my ass till it was red?

My Mudder

Who lifted me from my cozy cot

And put me on an ice cold pot,

And made me P if I could or not?

My Mudder

And when the morning lights had come.

And on my crib I dribbled some,

Who came and wiped my little bum?

My M.dder

Who did my hair so neatly part,

And press me gently to her heart

And sometimes squeeze me tii I tart?

My Mudder

TEN WAYS TO HANDLE STRESS

1 Pop some popcorn without putting the lid on!
2. When someone says "Have a Nice Day," tell them that you have other plans!
3. Put your kids clothes on backwards and send him off to school as if nothing was wrong!
4. Tattoo "Out to Lunch" on your forehead!
5. Leaf through a National Geographic and draw underwear on the natives!
6. Go shopping! Buy everything! Sweat in it and return it to the store the next day!
7. Sit naked on a shelled hard boiled egg!
8. Start a nasty rumor and see if you recognize it when it comes back to you!
9. Bill your doctor for the time spent in his waiting room!
10. Lie on your back eating celery ... using your navel as a salt dipper.

(768)

Dear Earthling.

Hi! I am a creature from outer space. I have transformed myself into a piece of paper. Right now I am having sex with your fingers. I know you like it because you are smiling. Please pass me on to someone else because I'm really horny.

GIRLS... TEAR *OUT* THIS PAGE AND HANG IT ON THE HEAD OF
YOUR BED... JUST GIVE YOUR HUSBAND A NUMBER!

1. I have a headache
2. My period
3. Back hurts
4. Too cold
5. Too hot
6. Your breath smells like beer
7. My breath smells like beer
8. Too early
9. Too late
10. I have to fix breakfast
11. I have to fix lunch
12. I have to fix supper
13. Forgot to take the pill
14. I've been ironing all day
15. Is that all you think of.?

16. The kids might hear us
17. Not in the bath tub
18. 1 don't like this position
19. 1 gave at the office
20. Slam the window on it
21. It's Monday
22. It's Tuesday
23. It's Wednesday
24. It's Thursday
25. It's Friday
26. It's Saturday
27. It's Sunday
28. Not here in the supermarket
29. It's no fun now that we're married
30. Stick it up your ...

(770)

My secretary quit today, amid a lot of strife, she sneaked back from the restroom and caught me with my wife!

(771)

DID YOU HEAR ABOUT ...

* The hillbilly who studied for five days because his doctor asked for a urine test!

* The wife who liked to talk to her husband when she was having sex? She only did it when there was a telephone handy!

* The city guy who milked a bull instead of a cow? He didn't get much milk, but he sure made a friend for life!

* The difference between a hog and a man? A hog don't have to sit in a bar all night and buy drinks just so he can screw a pig!

* What do they call syphilis in Russia? ROTYACROTCHOFF!

* Sex and how it was like a bridge game? You don't need a partner if you have a good hand!

* Breasts and toy trains ... I, now what they have in common? They were meant for kids, but their father's won't let them play with them.

* The guy who was feeling so low he got his face slapped!

* The guy who was so lazy he married a pregnant woman!

(continued on next page)

*   The guy who thought "Peter Pan" was something to put under the bed!

*   The guy who thought a sanitary belt was a drink from a clean shot glass!
*   What they call a white man with five black people? "Coach"

*   The elephant who looked at a naked man and said, "How in the world do you breathe out of that little thing?"

(772)

Trying to sell his new and totally remarkable computer to the youthful businessman, the inventor invited his skeptical client to ask it a question - any question. The executive sat down and typed out his query: "WHERE IS MY FATHER?"

The machine rapidly printed the reply: "YOUR FATHER IS FISHING IN MICHIGAN."

"This contraption doesn't know what it's talking about," bellowed the prospective customer. "My father's been dead for twenty years."

Certain that his creation was infallible, the scientist suggested, "Why don't you ask the same question in a different form?"

The chap then confidently typed: "WHERE IS MY MOTHER'S HUSBAND?" - to which the mechanical brain answered: "YOUR MOTHER'S HUSBAND HAS BEEN DEAD FOR TWENTY YEARS. YOUR FATHER HAS JUST LANDED A THREE-POUND TROUT!"

(773)

1 notice your daughter didn't get home until three o'clock this morning," said Mrs. Jones to Mrs. Brown across the back yard fence. "My daughter was in the house before midnight."

"I know," answered Mrs. Jones coolly, "But you see, my daughter walked home!"

(774)

After the honeymooners had gone down to breakfast, the hotel maid found a five-dollar bill pinned over a stain on the sheet. With the money was a note that read, "Sorry." The maid changed the linen and pinned a note on the pillow saying. "That's OK, come again!"

(775)

Sam and Al had been partners for many years and they shared and shared alike in almost everything, including the affection of their pliable and rather hot-blooded secretary. One morning Sam came into Al's office extremely upset.

"Al," he moaned, "something terrible has happened. Our secretary is going to have a baby. We are going to be a father."

But Al, who was the calmer of the two, sat his partner down and pointed out that a great many worse things could have happened to them; business could have fallen off, for instance. They agreed that the only thing to do was share and share alike, as they always had. They would see that their secretary got the very best in medical care, they decided, and after the child was born he would want for nothing. A room of his own, fine clothes and the best in schooling; they would set up a trust fund immediately after his birth to guarantee him a college education. The lucky youngster would have two fathers instead of just one.

And before they knew it, the big day had arrived. The two of them paced back and forth in the hospital waiting room, until Sam could stand it no longer.

"I'm too nervous up here," he said. "I'm going to go down and sit in the car. As soon as something happens, you come down and tell me."

Al agreed, and in less than an hour he was down on the street wearing a grave expression. It was obvious to Sam, even before his partner spoke, that something was wrong. "What's the matter?" Sam asked, starting to choke up. "Is it bad news??" His partner nodded. "We had twins," Al said, "and mine, died."

(776)
SPECIAL NOTICE

Subject: Increased Tax Payments for all Males
To: All Taxpayers
From: USA Internal Revenue Service

           Ruben J. Cutchepeckeroff, Director
           XVFI

President Clinton has issued a directive effective immediately. In effect, it states that he now wishes everything taxed, which shall now include your pecker. The directive explained that your pecker is now subject to taxation for the following reasons:
*   40% of the time it is hanging around unemployed
*   30% of the time it is pissed off
*   20% of the time it is hard up
*   10% of the time it operates in the hole

FURTHERMORE: It has two dependents, and they are both nuts!
     Accordingly, after February of 1996, your pecker will be taxed, based on its size, using the *PECKER CHECKER SCALE* below. You will be responsible for determining your own category and you must insert the additional tax to be collected under "Other Taxes," Page 2, Part V, Line 61 of your Standard Income Tax Return, (Form 1040).

PECKER CHECKER SCALE

10 to 12 inches	Luxury Tax	$50.00
08 to 10 inches	Pole Tax	$25.00
06 to 08 inches	Privilege Tax	$15.00
04 to 06 inches	Nuisance Tax	$ 5.00

NOTE;
*   Anyone under 04 inches is eligible for refund
*   Males in excess of 12 inches should file for "Capital Gain"
*   Do not apply for an extension as it will not be granted.

(777)

The young boy entered the living room of his home and sat down beside his mother. After a few minutes of deep thought, he said, "Mom, is it true that people can be taken apart like machines?"

"Of course not," his mother answered. "Where did you hear such nonsense?" "Well, just now, Daddy was talking to somebody on the phone," the lad continued, "and I heard him say that last night he screwed the ass off his secretary!.

(778)
SO YOU WANT TO BE THE BOSS!

When the body was first made, all parts wanted to be boss!

The Brain said: Since I control everything and do all the thinking, I should be Boss.

The Foot said: Since I carry man where he wants to go and get him in a position to do what the brain wants, I should be boss.

The Hands said: Since we must do all the work and earn all the money to keep the rest of you going, we should be boss.

The Eyes said: Since we must look out for all of you and tell you where danger lurks, we should be boss.

And so it went with the heart, the ears, the lung,, and finally the asshole. The asshole said, "why shouldn't I be boss?" All the other parts of the body laughed and laughed at the idea of an asshole being boss. The Asshole was so angered that he blocked himself off and refused to function. Soon the brain was feverish, the eyes crossed and ached, the feet were too weak to walk, the hands hung limply at the sides, and the heart and lungs struggled to keep going. All the parts of the body pleaded with the brain to relent and let the asshole be the boss. And so it happened! All the parts of the body did all the work and the asshole just bossed and passed gas wherever he went.

MORAL: You don't have to have a Brain to be Boss ... just an Asshole!

CONFUCIUS SAYS

1. Baby conceived on back seat of car with automatic transmission grows
   up to be shiftless bastard.
2. Man who lay girl on hill not on level.
3. Man who have titty in mouth make clean breast of things.
4. He who fishes in other man's well often catches crabs.
5. Wife who puts man in dog house may find him in cat house.
6. Boy who plays with himself pulls boner.
7. Girl who douches with vinegar walk around with sour puss.
8. Wife who slides down banister make monkey shine.
9. Virgin like balloon: One prick --- all gone.
10. Girl who goes to bed with detective must kiss dick.
11. Woman who puts rooster in freezer have frozen cock.
12. Man who sells kotex is crack salesman.
13. Blonde girl have black hair by cracky.
14. Boy who goes to bed with sex problem on mind wakes up with solution
15. Girl should not marry basketball player - he dribbles before he shoots.
16. Man who screws cook in pantry sometimes get ass in jam.
17. Woman who cooks carrots and peas in same pot is very unsanitary.
18. Kotex not best thing in world, but next to it.
19. Man who plays with titty get bust in mouth.
20. Woman who springs on innerspring this summer get offspring next spring.
21. Squirrel lay on rock and crack nuts: Man lay on crack and rock nuts.
22. Woman pilot who fly upside down have crack-up.
23. Better to sleep with old hen than pullet.
24. Man who lets fart in church must sit in own pew.
25. Man who marries girl with no bust have right to feel low down.
26. Man with athletic finger make broad jump.
27. Man who plays golf in rain gets balls wet.

20 TYPES OF PEOPLE YOU MIGHT MEET
IN THE MEN'S ROOM!

EXCITABLE: Shorts half twisted around, cannot find hole, rips shorts.

SOCIABLE: joins friends in piss whether he has to or not.

CROSS-EYED: Look into next urinal to see how the other guy is fixed.

TIMID: Cannot piss if someone is watching, flushes urinal, comes back later.

INDIFFERENT: All urinals being used, pisses in sink.

CLEVER: No hands, fixes tie, looks around and usually pisses on floor.

WORRIED: Not sure of where he has been lately, makes quick inspection.

FRIVOLOUS: Plays stream up, down and across urinals, tries to hit fly or bug.

ABSENT-MINDED: Opens vest, pulls out tie, pisses in pants.

CHILDISH: Pisses directly in bottom of urinal, likes to see it bubble.

SNEAK: Farts silently while pissing, acts very innocent, knows man in next stall will get blamed.

PATIENT: Stands very close for a long while waiting, reads with free hand.

DESPERATE: Waits in long line, teeth floating, pisses in pants.

TOUGH: Bangs dick on side of urinal to dry it.

EFFICIENT: Waits until he has to crap, then does both.

FAT: Backs up and takes a blind shot at urinal, pisses in shoe.

LITTLE: Stands on box, falls in, drowns.

DRUNK: Holds left thumb in right hand, pisses in pants.

DISGRUNTLED: Stands for a while, gives up, walks away.

CONCEITED: Holds two inch dick like a baseball bat.

(781)

"A baby was born last night at the hospital with no tallywhacker." "What do they do in a case like that?" "Wait until she's 18 years old and insert one!"

(782)

The drunk sat at the bar with three dark brown pellets in his hand. The bartender asked what they were, and the drunk said, "These are smart pills ... they make you smart." So the bartender said, "Let me have one," and he downed it with water. Persistently he came back and said, "I don't feel any smarter," so the drunk said, "Have another," which he did. Later the bartender asked for a third, which he smelled, tasted and said, "This tastes like sheep manure." And the drunk replied, "My God, it's working! You are starting to get smarter! "

(783)

He snuggled up to his wife and begged for a little loving, but she rebuked him, saying, "Don't talk about loving where the children can hear ... just ask me if you can use my washing machine." So in a night or two SHE was the one who had the urge, and she snuggled over and sighed, "Dear, would you like to use my washing machine?" and he replied, "No, love, I only had a small bundle tonight, so I used the hand laundry......"

(784)

I'm trying to raise an orphan calf. It's kind of hard to teach one to take a bottle. While they're learning, they'll grab onto just about anything and start sucking . . . a finger, water hose, or whatever will fit in their mouths. Today while I was in the pen, she grabbed one of my thumbs between her lips, and she was so gentle with it, her tongue felt so soft and warm, I got an idea. The idea was "I bet you are thinking dirty!"

(785)

The old Texas rancher and his wife, both far exceeding by weight any normal people, sat at the bar. A couple of fellows got into an argument about how two people so obese could make with a piece, and finally one got up enough courage to ask the fat rancher how he worked it in at home. The rancher looked at him more in sorrow than in anger, and replied, "You're the third little dick today who has asked me that question!"

(786)

The old farmer, married to a teenage wife, was having beddie-bye trouble, since he was so tired in the evening. He went to a doctor who advised him to take his shotgun to the field with him. "Then, in the mornings, when you are fresh, and get an urge, shoot your gun three times as a signal to your wife. She can come running and you can make out with her right there between the rows." So the farmer went and tried this, and several weeks later ran into the doctor on the street. "How did it work out?" said the Doc. "Fine for a while," said the old farmer, "But then the hunting season opened and I haven't seen her since."

(787)

Friends may come and friends may go
And friends may peter out, you know,
But we'll be friends through thick and thin,
Peter out or peter in!

(788)

She married the poor fellow who lost a foot in the war, then wrote her mama, "Jim is a wonderful fellow, but he only has one foot." And the old lady wrote back, "You should be so lucky... I married your old man and he only had five inches!"

Two little girls about six, put on their mother's clothes, high heels and all, went down to the comer drug store and climbed up on the soda fountain stools. One said, "I think I'll have a strawberry sundae with nuts." The other kid thought a minute and said, "I think I'll have a douche... mother says they're refreshing!"

Did you hear about the thrifty cat ? Twice a week he puts something in the kitty!

The prostitute told the Texas farmer, "I make it a practice to never go to bed with anyone who doesn't have at least a twelve inch peter." The farmer replied, "That's BS I'm not about to cut off two inches for anybody !"

Did you hear about Blitzen the brown nosed reindeer ? He could run just as fast as Rudolph. He just couldn't stop as fast !

Something to think about ! Do you realize that every joke in this book is just like sex ? No fun if don't get it !

(794)

The executive walked into the office on Monday morning. His secretary said, "Before you get to your desk, I have some good news and some bad news for you ." "Which do you want first ?" The executive replied "How about the good news first." "OK ," She said, "The good news is that you are not sterile." Now, "Are you ready for the bad news ?"

(795)

How about the guy who was really 'shook up' He told his friend, I've been uptight before but I haven't been this uptight since Donna Marie asked me what I wanted to name the baby." His friend replied, "What's so bad about that?" The 'shook up' one stammered, "Donna Marie is my secretary !"

(796)

Then there was the one about the drunk who went to the doctor and told him he wanted a "penis transplant!" The doctor informed him that a black twelve incher would cost him three thousand dollars. The drunk shook his head and asked, "How much does a white one cost ?" To which the doctor replied, "That size doesn't come in white !"

(797)

Do you know how to get a hippie out of the bathtub ? Just turn on the water.......

(798)

"You were very bashful before you married Mom, eh, Pop ?" The little boy asked his pappy. "What makes you ask that ?" Said his father. The boy said, "Well, Mom told me if you hadn't been so bashful, I'd be two years older !"

(799)

"My roommate has the cutest idea ! He takes cherry pop, fills up some rubbers with it, ties a knot in them and then puts them in the freezer....a few hours latter, guess what, cockicles !"

(800)

Important Notice from the Civil Defense: In case of nuclear attack, crawl under a large, heavy table, draw your knees up by your ears, put your head between your legs and kiss your butt goodbye!

(801)

A body is rolled into the Funeral home with a penis that measured eleven inches long. The Assistant Mortician calls over to his boss and says "Have you ever seen one like this ?" "Sure," Says the boss. "In fact , I have one like that myself." "You do ?" stammers the assistant. "Really, an eleven incher ?" "No." Replied the Mortician. "Dead."

(802)

Two fellows were standing side by side at the urinals in the men's room at the Hotel Eden Roc in Miami Beach. One tuned to the other and said, "You were circumcised by Rabbi Schleimie Heiselsplitz, weren't you." And the other man said, "Why, yes! How did you know ?" And the first fellow replied, "I happen to remember he always cuts on a bias, and you have just peed all over my left shoe!"

(803)

Mrs. Jensen was waiting to see the doctor when there was a big commotion, and out ran a nun, screaming. The doctor said, "You're next," and Mrs. Jensen said, "I'm not sure I want to be after the way that nun was acting ... just what did you do to her?" The doctor answered, "I didn't do anything to her... I just told her she was pregnant." Mrs. Jensen, most surprised said, "Well, WAS SHE?" And the doctor said, "Of course not, but it sure cured her hiccups!"

(804)

The pretty young school teacher was concerned about one of her eleven year-old students. Taking him aside after class one day, she asked, "Victor, why has your school work been so poor lately?" "I can't concentrate," replied the lad. "I'm afraid I've fallen in love." "Is that so?" said the teacher, holding back an urge to smile. "And with whom?" "With you," he answered. "But Victor," exclaimed the secretly pleased young lady, "don't you see how silly that is? It's true that I would like a husband of my own someday, but I don't want a child." "Oh, don't worry," said Victor 'I'll steal some of Mom's birth control pills!"

(805)

A vacuum cleaner salesman called on a housewife out in a rural area. She said she wasn't interested, but he wouldn't leave without giving a demonstration. So she finally snapped, "Do your dumb thing." He ran out to the corral, brought in a bushel of droppings, and spread them all over the floor. "Now," he boasted, "I'll turn on my sweeper, and if it doesn't suck up all those horse apples, I'll eat them myself." The lady sighed, "Well, I sure hope you're hungry, Mister, we don't have electricity here!"

(806)

A man taking a sex survey asked a housewife if she ever had relations during the daytime. She told him she enjoyed several such times a week. He said, "Fine. Now can I talk to your husband about it?" She replied, "I'd rather you didn't... he doesn't know it yet!"

(807)

While watching the youngsters dance, one chaperone remarked to another, "We did the same thing when I was in school... only we called it foreplay!"

(808)

Jim Jones went over to Sam Brown's to buy a rooster. The neighbor wasn't home, so Mrs. Brown look care of the transaction. She quoted $2 but Jim had only a $10 bill, so he said he'd pay later. Several days later he ran into Sam in town, and said, "By the way, Sam, here's $2 for that cock I got from your wife," and Sam gazed steadily at Jim for a few seconds and replied, "You really know how to hurt a guy, my conscience really bothers me. I never gave your wife anything!"

(809)

Two call girls were in a bar discussing the events of last night over martinis. "How did you make out with that eccentric millionaire ?" asked one. "He was really spooky," said the other. "He gave a hundred bucks, but it wasn't worth it." The first asked why. "He wanted to make love in a COFFIN!" the other said. "No kidding! I'll bet that really shook you up!" The millionaire's girlfriend replied, "Yes, it sure did, but you should have seen the look on the faces of the six pall bearers!"

(810)

Two old maids walked along the dark street late at night, and noticed two sailors walking along behind them. Said one old maid, "Aren't those sailors out after hours?" And the other replied, "I sure hope so."

(811)

The teacher told the three little boys to go home and look at TV and learn something new about sex. So they came back the next day and Billy said, "I watched Ben Casey and learned a lot." And Bobby said, "I watched Night Nurse and learned a lot." And Johnny said, "I watched Gene Autrey kill eight Indians." The teacher said, "You didn't learn very much about sex from that," and Johnny said, "Oh, I don't know... it sure taught eight Indians not to screw around with Gene Autrey!"

(812)

Farmer Farkleberry bought a young bull. When he arrived he ran out, started running around from one cow to the other, entranced with all this new material to work on. The old bull, who had been there for years, started snorting and pawing the ground, so Farmer Farkleberry said, "Why are you kicking up the dirt... you can't do anything about it!" The old bull replied, "I can let him know I'm not a cow, can't I?"

(813)

The lady was desperate..."My husband is very run down and pays me NO mind, doctor," she said. "Please give me something to build him up." The doctor was confidential, "Well, Mrs. Ross, there is a brand of dog food that is just great to build up the viability and virility of a man ... just take the labels off the cans and he'll never know the difference." Two months later the doc called Mrs. Ross to learn the outcome and she said, "My husband died, but it wasn't your fault. Bless his poor soul, the dog food worked wonders for him, but one day he broke his neck, twisting himself around and licking his peter!"

(814)

An attendant took the inmates of a mental asylum to a ball game. When they played the national anthem at the start of the game, he hollered, "STAND, NUTS!' and they all stood obediently. When the music stopped, he hollered "SIT, NUTS!" and they all sat. What really messed everything up was when the man came around hollering "PEANUTS!" That's when the usher threw us out of the ball park!

(815)

A lady on train was working a crossword puzzle and got stumped. She asked the man next to her, "Do you know a four-letter word, ending in 'I-T' that you'll find at the bottom of a bird cage?" So the man said, "Yes, GRIT." And the lady said, "Do you have a pencil with an eraser on the end?"

(816)

A pregnant woman's husband tried to get some. She asked, "Can't you wait until after the baby comes?" He groaned, "It will be 12 years before the kid is old enough to do that ..."

(817)

A show girl filed a paternity suit against a prominent sports figure. The jury stared at the clean-cut young man and decided he just couldn't get a woman in trouble and refused to do right by her. So they ruled he wasn't the one who done it. On hearing the verdict, the athlete turned to his lawyer and said, "I understand this means I don't have to pay, but they didn't mention visitation rights. When do I get to see my kid?"

(818)

Bill and Mary had been seeing a lot of each other. One evening while waiting for Mary to dress, Bill was approached by her little brother, who asked, "Can my sister trust you not to get fresh?" Bill blushed, "Why Tommy, where did you get such a question?" Tommy responded, "I heard her tell my mama if she could be sure of that, she'd save a fortune on birth control pills."

(819)

A fellow went into a gun shop and asked to see a 357 mg. Rifle. The owner asked, "What do you plan to shoot with a gun that big?" The man answered, "Cans." The owner said, "Well, I can sell you a 22 rifle that'll do just as good. What kind of cans are you going to shoot?" He growled, "The ones on the S.O.B's I find on top of my wife!"

(820)

While dancing at Roseland, a man assayed small talk with his partner. "Honey, do you know the minuet?" "Hell no," she replied, "I don't even know the men I've laid!"

(821)

My boyfriend finally popped the question, but I said no...not until after we're married!"

(822)

The hitchhiker kept saying it wasn't right to do it without a rubber, but the trucker insisted his vasectomy operation would make everything okay. Finally she gave in. Later, as he dropped her off, the lying S.O.B. grinned, "By the way honey, I didn't mean everything I said. If your belly starts to swell, you might look me up ... but don't expect to find me." She drawled, "That's all right, because I didn't say everything I meant ... I have an appointment tomorrow at the VD clinic!"

(823)

A guy picks up a woman in a bar. She takes him back to her place and they go to bed. He climbs on top of her and starts pumping away.
"Is it in yet?"
"Yes, it is."
"Are you sure?"
"Sure I'm sure. If you don't believe me, look for yourself." He leans back so she can see.
"Well, I guess you're right," she admits, "but I must say that's the smallest organ I've ever seen."
"Believe me, lady, I had no idea I'd be playing in the Mormon tabernacle!"

(824)

BANANA NUT BREAD

2 whole nuts
1 large banana
2 arms
2 well-shaped legs
1 fur lined mixing bowl
2 milk containers
2 laughing eyes

Look into eyes and part legs; gently squeeze milk containers until mixing bowl is well greased. Add banana and work in-and-out until well greased. Cover with nuts and sigh with relief. When cake is done, set on porch and cool. Be sure to wash bowl and mixer.

DO NOT LICK BOWL!

(825)

The old maid told the burglar she didn't have any money, then gasped as he made a tentative search. "You'd better give me your money now." he said menacingly, "or I'm going to *really* search you!" "But I don't have any!" she protested, almost in tears. So he *really* searched her. "I guess you were on the level," he finally muttered angrily, "you don't have any money on you." "For heaven's sake," she wailed, "don't stop now. I'll write you a check!"

(826)

SECRET LOVE
Once I had a secret love,
In a nylon negligee.
Afterwards, my secret love
Said I didn't have to pay.
So I asked the friendly whore
Why she gave her love to me.
She said, "Mister, don't be sore
Feely Mattress pays my fee."
Now I'm shouting 'cause she wrecked my life,
Yesterday at 1: 15, my wife
Saw our scene on Channel Four,
And my secret love's no secret anymore!

(827)

As the nurse in the jungle hospital passed a heavily bandaged patient, she noticed that something was bothering him. Looking around, she saw a fly on top of the one protruding object that wasn't completely covered, so she said, "Wait till I get my fly swatter, and I'll knock it off." The patient replied, "Never mind, if that fly makes one more round, it will come off real fast!"

(828)

One morning a newly wed young man entered the Confessional and said, "Father, I want to confess. I had intercourse with my wife ten times last night." The priest said, "But that's no sin." The young man replied, "I know, Father, but gee whiz, I just HAD to tell somebody!"

(829)

Do you know what your wife told the lady next door? "My husband is one of the original movie cartoon heroes. He's built like Superman and hung line Mighty Mouse."

(830)

100 young ladies were enrolling in a Girls School. The Headmistress called them all together and said, "Rumor has it a man is hiding somewhere in the building." 99 students gasped, one giggled. "Also," the Headmistress continued, "The rumor states that this intruder has been seducing one of our young ladies." 99 students gasped, one giggled. "Furthermore, the Headmistress said, "I found a condom on the floor last night, and it had a great big hole in it." 99 students giggled, one fainted!

(831)

A concrete finisher consulted a doctor about his constipation, and the doc gave him a laxative. He came back three days later, with no results, so the doctor prescribed a more potent remedy. Several more days passed, but nothing else did, so he returned to the doctor again. This time the doctor said, "There's nothing really wrong with you. Take off your pants and bend over." So he did, and the doctor gave him a tremendous whack across the rump with a table leaf, and the stuff came forth, all over the office. When he could speak again, the man said, "Gosh, doc, I hope I don't have to get hit like that every time I have to go!" The doctor replied, "You won't, if you stop using those cement bags for toilet paper!"

(832)

At Show and Tell, little Bobby informs the class that his mother has an imaginary friend. "Are you sure about that, Bobby?" the teacher says. "That's very unusual for a grown-up." "Yeah, she does," says Bobby, "and his name is Hugh." "Really?" "Yep. At night Mommy and Daddy go into their bedroom all by themselves. They bounce around the bed for a while, and Mommy asks, "Did Hugh come yet?"

(833)

The traveling salesman put his arm around the bellhop's shoulders and whispered, "Call me a whore, buddy." The bellhop replied, " okay, handsome, you're a whore. How much do you want for a blow job?"

(834)

THE STORY OF LIFE
When things fall flat,
As they often will;
Your road is rocky
And straight up hill;
Your money is low
And prices are steep;
You try to laugh,
But instead you weep;
You're caught by the balls
And held in a trap ...
Don't turn to me.
I don't give a crap.

(835)

A traveling salesman consulted his doctor, complaining of a general rundown condition. The doctor took note of his occupation and asked right off, "How often do you have sex?" The salesman replied, "Every Monday, Wednesday, Friday and Saturday." The doctor frowned and said, "That's a little too frequent. Why don't you cut out Saturdays?" The salesman said, "I can't do that, Doctor. It's the only night of the week I'm home with my wife."

(836)

Bachelor Bill sat down at his desk, wrote out checks for the car payment, stereo payment, TV payment, and the monthly installments on his department store charge cards. Then he walked into the bathroom, hauled out his muscle, aimed it at the toilet, patted it lovingly on the head, and said, "This is the only thing I own that's paid for... and it leaks."

(837)

As an old man lay dying, he whispered to his nurse, "In my pocket you willl find a name and address. "Cough, cough." Please let her know that I have gone. Tell her I loved her right up to the end. "Cough, Cough." And I would also be happy if you would notify my wife!"

(838)

When the groom commented on his bride's inner spaciousness, she explained, "I broke my hymen sliding down a pole." He asked suspiciously, "Are you sure?" "No not really," she replied, "It could have been a German or maybe a Mexican!"

(839)

A big old black grizzly bear escaped from the circus and was standing on main street, holding onto a lamp post. Leroy, who was really bombed out, walked up and gave the bear a big hug. The bear grabbed a hold of Leroy and hit him so hard it almost killed him. Just before the Medics arrived, Leroy whimpered, "Well, that's the way it goes, you give a lady of the night a new fur coat, and she thinks she owns the town."

(840)

A pesky fence salesman stopped by the farm one day while Aunt Helen was home alone, and refused to leave until she bought something. Aunt Helen finally lost her temper and snapped, "okay, give me enough barb wire to reach from the top of your head to the tip of your peter. He wrote up the order and left, but next week a whole trainload of barb wire arrived, so Uncle Homer phoned the man and asked what happened. The fellow answered, "Ges Mister, I forgot to tell your wife... my folks didn't immigrate until I'd been circumcised, and the tip of my peter is in Bangkok !"

(841)

Then there was this dummy who was always being picked on by his coworkers at the factory ! One day they put a sign on his back and he never knew it was there. The sign read, "Kick my butt!" Everywhere the poor guy would go, someone would come up behind him and give him a big kick. After about three hours, he was no where to be found, but one of the workers found him in the restroom and the poor soul was sticking a stick of dynamite up his back end. His friend asked him, "What in hell are you doing?" The dummy replied, "I'm getting damn tired of being kicked in the butt, the next bastard that does it will get his foot blown off!"

(842)

Sam had been a soldier at war for more than three years, during which he had been in many battles and won many decorations. He was finally discharged from service and returned home to a wife and son whom he hadn't seen in almost four years.

As he was walking up the path to his house, his young son spotted him and yelled, "Mommy, Mommy, here comes Daddy, and he's got a purple heart on!" to which the mother replied, "I don't give a damn what color it is! Let him in, and you go play at the Jones' for a couple of hours!"

(843)

And then there's the little boy who got up at midnight to go to the bathroom and passed his parent's bedroom. Noticing that the door was opened, he walked in and saw his mother performing fellatio on his father.

The boy walked out of the bedroom scratching his head and muttering. "And they sent *me* to the doctor for sucking my thumb!"

(844)

A pole was suffering from constipation, so his doctor prescribed suppositories. A week later the Pole complained to the doctor that they didn't produce the desired results. "Have you been taking them regularly?" the doctor asked. "What do you think I've been doing," the Pole said, "shoving them up my ass?"

(845)

Then there was this pregnant Indian girl who walked into the family teepee and said to her Mom and Dad, "How." The old man snapped back, "We both know how, dumb ass, what we want to know is WHO?"

(846)

MARY HAD A LITTLE THING, THAT ALWAYS WANTED SOME
AND EVERYWHERE THAT MARY WENT, HER THING WAS SURE
TO
COME!

(847)

Have you heard about the egotistical "stud" who gave his girlfriend a Microwave oven for Christmas? She thanked him and said, "Gee, just what I need, one more thing that heats up instantly and goes "ding" in about twenty seconds!"

(848)

Two beautiful, sexy coeds in the band room at college. One said to the other, "Helen Patricia, do you remember the 'Minuet ?" "Are you kidding, honey," Helen Patricia replied, "I can't hardly remember the ones I had sex with!"

(849)

JENNIE: "Have you ever tried grass?"
JEANNIE: "Yes, but I prefer to do it on a water mattress!"

(850)

The little boy raised his hand and asked the teacher if he could leave the room for a moment. She said, "Yes, Jimmy, if you'll say your ABC's for me," so Jimmy swiftly ratted off A-B-C-D-E-F-G-H-I-J-K,-L-M-N-O-Q-R-S-T-U-V-W-X-Y-Z." "That's pretty good," said the teacher, "But where was the P?" And Jimmy answered, "With all this silly delay, it's now running down my leg!"

(851)

A woman heard a hen squawking, so she looked out the kitchen window. Her little son had the old hen on his lap and was looking all through the feathers. She cried, "What are you doing to the old hen?" The little boy said, "Looking for tits." The mother laughed, "Chickens don't have tits..... whatever gave you that idea?" The son replied, "When I was down at Daddy's office, I heard him tell his secretary, "If my old hen had tits like you got, she'd *be some chicken!"*

(852)

An ironing board salesman was sleeping in an upper berth on the train, and had his ironing board sample with him. He kept whispering to a sweet young thing who was sleeping across the aisle from him to "Come on over here with me." Finally she said, "How will I get over there?" and he whispered back, "Just slide over on THIS." And the fellow in the bottom berth, who had been listening snarled out, "Oh yeah? How is she going to get back again?"

(853)

Sally came home and caught her roommate, Millie in bed with a young man. "Goodness gracious!" screamed Sally, what WOULD your mother say, Millie, if she found out about this?" Millie smiled and replied, "She'd RAISE HELL, he's HER boyfriend!"

(854)

The fifth grade class was studying Indians, and the teacher asked if anyone in the room was part Indian. One little boy raised his hand and said he was half Indian. The teacher asked, "What tribe?" The boy replied, "It wasn't a whole tribe, ma'am. It was just one brave that came through with a carnival."

(855)

He got on a very crowded street car and grabbed a strap for the long trip to the suburbs. Beans for lunch had him under great pressure and finally he let one that was so bad it peeled the paint off the street car. Then, trying to be nonchalant, he asked a man sitting by the window, "Do you have a newspaper?" and the man answered, "No, but I'll grab a hand full of leaves for you off the next tree we pass by ..... "

(856)

The judge came home and found his wife in bed with his very best friend.
"Hey, what do you think, you're doing?" "See," the wife said to the man beside her, "I told you he was stupid!"

(857)

Inflation was getting out of hand so Joe suggested to his wife, Louise, that they try a unique way to save some money on the side. "Every time I lay you, I'll give you a dollar for your piggy bank," he said. A few weeks later, they decided to open the piggy bank. Out tumbled a bunch of dollars, but these were mixed with a rich cluster of five's, tens and twenties. "Louise," asked Joe, "where did you get all that money? Each time we screwed I only gave you a dollar." "So?" she said. "Do you think everyone is as stingy as you?"

(858)

Doris had the most beautiful breasts Don had ever seen. His desire to see them fully exposed was his number one passion. Finally he approached Doris and said, "I'll give you $ 100 if you'll take off your blouse and let me kiss your nipples." Doris, who was always broke, agreed and proceeded to take off her blouse and bra. Don stared so hard that a wet spot suddenly blossomed on his trouser. "Well, what are you waiting for?" Asked Doris, "don't you have the nerve?" " I don't have the $ 100, " sighed Don.

(859)

Three men and a woman were ship wrecked on a desert isle. After two weeks the woman was so ashamed of what she was doing she killed herself. Two weeks later, the men were so ashamed of what they were doing, they buried her.......... a week later the men were so ashamed of what they were doing they dug her up again......

(860)

"This year we gave the Postman $25 for Christmas. When I asked the girl next door what she gave him, she answered, " a piece of tail." I asked her how she could do such a thing, and she said, "I asked my husband what to give the mailman, and he said, "oh, screw the mailman!" So I did!"

(861)

The Kindergarten teacher held up a big picture and said, "What's this?" One kid said, "That's a horse." Then she held up another picture and another kid said, "That's a cow." Then she held up a picture of a big buck deer, said, What's this?" Silence. Then the teacher said, "What does your Mommy call your call your Daddy when they wake up in the mornings?" More silence. Finally a kid far back spoke up and said . . . "I know teacher, "that's a horny bastard!"

(862)

As the high school teacher passed out the first report cards of the year to the freshman class, she noticed one blonde, overblown young lady was scowling. "What's the matter . . . , aren't you satisfied with your marks, Patty.?" The teacher asked. "I certainly am NOT," cried Patty. "You gave me an 'F' in sex ... and I didn't even know I was taking it!"

(863)

The upstairs maid was quitting to get married. The lady of the house, who had just divorced her own husband warned, "Marriage isn't all tender caresses. It gets harder than you think. Do you know the fellow well enough to spend your whole life together?" The maid said, "Yes mum, I do. After all, I worked here all those years YOU were married to him!"

(864)

A wolf asked the innocent young lamb who worked in his office if she'd like to share a hotel room in Las Vegas for two weeks. Mother had warned her that all proposals didn't include marriage, so she asked warily, "Would we go to the church first?" He gave her a puzzled look and said, "Hell no, you ninny . . . with all those dice tables, who wants to play Bingo!"

(865)

NOTE TO BRIDEGROOMS

Don't embarrass your new wife by asking her about her past performances.

Wait until the morning after the wedding and hand her a five-dollar bill. If she asks, "What is this for?" She was a virgin.

(866)

Two housewives were exchanging confidential secrets. One woman whispered, "Last week I caught my husband with his secretary, and she was taking a lot more than notes. To punish the rat, I made him buy me a new dress." Her friend asked, "Did you also have him fire the girl? She answered, "No, not yet... I still need a mink coat!"

(867)

The shapely coed stepped out of the shower when she noticed a puzzled look on her roommate's face. "Do you know there's the impression of a large "M" on your stomach?" The roommate asked. "My fiancee's in town this weekend," confided the young thing "and he likes to make love with his football letter sweater on." "Which school does he attend, Michigan or Minnesota?" questioned her friend. "Neither," giggled the first girl, "He goes to Wisconsin!"

(868)

In a Pennsylvania coal town, a young man went down to the draft board for his pre-induction physical. He started to roll back his foreskin for the short arm search, and something fell out. The medic asked, "What was that?" The youth explained, "My chewing gum. I work in the mines, and when I get tired of chewing, that's the only clean place to park it." He skinned back a little farther, and another wad dropped out. Again the doc inquired, "What's that?" The draftee said, "That's my buddy's gum... he's circumcised!"

(869)

Officer Homer Tucker brought a scared young pair into the station house and reported, "I caught these two creeps screwing in the park. I want them booked for indecent exposure, corrupting public morals, disturbing the peace, littering and polluting the ecology . And be quick about it. I've got to get my girlfriend out of the house before my wife comes home!"

(870)

A bunch of middle-aged couples were yakking it up over cocktails. Lance pulled that old gag, "I used to do it all night, but now it takes me all night to do it." Lance's wife screamed, "Hush up, I'm getting embarrassed!" Lance said, "I don't see why. I'm sure as hell not getting any at home!"

(871)

Dumb Hans met a French girl on an ocean cruise. Later, Hans told his friends, "We couldn't speak the same language, so we used our pocket dictionaries to talk. After a while she pulled me into her cabin, stripped to the buff, jerked off all my clothes, turned down the bed covers, and... there I stood, without my dictionary, not having the faintest notion what to say or do!"

(872)

The Master of Ceremonies introduced the main speaker by announcing, "Our Main Speaker tonight is without a peer . . . " Before he could continue, a lady in the front row hollered "That's awful! Did he get it shot off during the war?"

(873)

Homer was worried when he came home to find the house locked and dark, so he went to see if the lady next door knew where his wife was. It turned out that the lady next door was no lady, and before he knew it, there was dirty work going on at the crossroads. All of a sudden, he looked up from what he was doing, and cried, " What about your husband ? Won't he be home any minute now ?" The lady laughed, Don't worry about him. He's over at your house. "

(874)

The talk at the Gent's Club turned to adultery. Mike Casey sneered "I'll bet any man in this room a brand new hat that he's cheated on his wife at least once since their marriage." Bill Hock, popped up, "I'll take that wager!" Mike asked suspiciously, "How long have you been married?" Bill replied, "Almost three days." This tickled Mike so much that he ran home to tell his wife. She listened closely and then said, 'Ha ha, very funny... but where *is your* new hat?!

(875)

A second grade school teacher announced to her class that today would be farm animal day. "All right, children," she said. "What sound does a cow make?" "I know I know." Said Jimmy, "Moo!" "Very good, Jimmy," said the teacher. "And what sound does a chicken make ? " "Cluck, cluck! " cried Cindy. "Very good, Cindy," said the teacher. "Now, does anyone know, what sound a pig makes ?" Suddenly, little Eddie jumped up and down excitedly. "I know! I know ! " He shouted. "Stop or I'll shoot!"

A barber suspects that his wife is cheating on him, so one day he comes home early and catches her in bed with another man. "Aha!" he roars and leaps forward with his straight razor flashing. He slices off the guy's dick while it's still inside his wife. She starts screaming hysterically, "The man's bleeding, get some bandages!" The guy looks down and yells, "Bandages, hell! Get me a corkscrew!"

An old man walks into the William Morris Agency. From a suitcase he pulls a miniature Steinway grand piano. From his jacket pocket he pulls a perfectly formed human being, dressed in a tux with tails. The little man sits at the little piano and proceeds to beautifully play Chopin. Liszt, Rachmaninoff, and for an encore, Joplin. The agent says "That's great, it's wonderful, I can book this act anywhere. Where did you find it?" The old man answers, "I was clearing out my attic when I came across an old lamp. I thought if it was cleaned off I could get a few bucks for it. A genie popped out and granted me one wish." "And you wished for a twelve-inch pianist?" "Not exactly!"

You have no idea how my wife's relatives can eat. One year I bent over to say Grace and when I looked up again, somebody was handing me an after dinner mint!

If you ever want to make a lot of money as a prostitute, all you have to do is stand on a corner near an "X" rated movie house. You can be sure your customers will come a lot faster!

(880)

Ivan and Lickma stepped into the Fortune Teller's booth at the County Fair. The seeress gazed at Ivan's palm and intoned, "You are a happily married man. You have three children." LickMa chortled, "Ha Ha, you're wrong! We only have two." The fortune teller took a closer look at Ivan's hand and murmured, "you also believe, what your wife don't know can't hurt her!"

(881)

The undertaker came home, poured himself a stiff drink and told his wife, "I had one helluva experience today. The hotel manager called and said they'd found a dead couple locked in love's embrace in one of their -rooms, and would I please come measure and quietly get them out of there, as it was bad for business. Besides, they had another reservation for the room in 15 minutes. So I hurried on down, reeled out my tape and started to measure, head to toe, and across the back. Then I tried to pry them apart. Whew! What a struggle!" The wife asked, "Rigor mortis?" He shuddered, "Worse than that " I was in the wrong room!"

(882)

Homer Fudpucker invented a new cocktail that guarantees a "sack in the hay... he takes slow gin, rum and vodka and pours it into a 6 oz. glass of apple cider. The last time his girlfriend drank three, he finally came up with a name ... he calls it "Mounting Brew."

(883)

The sexy coed was being interviewed for a job and the personnel man asked her, "How far did you go in school? She blushed and replied, "Well, 90 percent of the time, I went all the way!"

(884)

Did you hear about the guy who promised his girlfriend a Hammond Organ for her birthday. "that's exactly what he gave her... a 10 pound ham and a 6-inch organ!

(885)

Someone told St. Peter about the survey that was taken which proved that 95 percent of the world's people were committing adultery. St. Peter decided it would be a nice idea to send the 5 percent a letter of appreciation. Know what the letter said . . . "you mean you didn't get one?"

(886)

The beautiful, dumb country doll married a city slicker, and he then trained her right He showed her what his nightingale was for, and Convinced her he was the only one in the world who had one. Things went well until one day he came home from work and she said, "I thought yours was the only one in the world, but your brother was by here and he had one, too." The fellow thought fast and said, " That was because I had two, and gave him one." The dumb wife replied, "Then why did you give him the big one?"

(887)

"Isn't the moon lovely?" she sighed. "If you say so," answered her date. "Personally, I'm in no position to say!"

(888)

The little boy pointed to two dogs in the park, and asked his father what they were doing. "They're making puppy's son," the father said. That night, the boy wondered into his parents' bedroom while they were in the process of making love. Asked what they were doing, the father replied, "making you a baby brother." "Gee Pop," the boy pleaded, "why don't you turn her over, I'd rather have a puppy!"

(889)

Complaining of the distance between campus buildings, the veterinarian's daughter wrote home for money to buy a bicycle. By the time she received the money, she had lost interest in the bicycle and she decided to buy a pet monkey instead. After a few weeks, the animal began losing its hair. Hoping her father might know a cure, she wrote, "all the hair is failing off my monkey... what shall I do?" Two days later came the terse reply ..."sell the bicycle!"

(890)

Before retiring on his wedding night, the young Minister turned to his sweet bride and said... "pardon me, darling. I'm going to pray for guidance." "Sweetheart," his wife answered, "I'll take care of the guidance. You pray for endurance."

(891)

Memo from Secretary to her boss ... "My reason for resigning will soon become apparent.......and, so will I."

(892)

Two little old ladies were chatting over the backyard fence. The first once boasted, "I went out with old man Cain last night, and I had to slap him twice." Her friend asked, "To stop him?" She giggled, "No... I had to wake him up to get him started!"

(893)

A young college student appeared at his draft board one morning wrapped in the American Flag. As he entered, he proclaimed at the top of his voice, "No matter what happens, don't hold up my induction! Let me start now and you can complete my papers later! I don't need a physical! I don't need a uniform, basic training, guns or anything! Just lemme' at the enemy! I'll kill them with my bare hands! If they shoot me, I'll get up and keep on going! I'll rip their barbed wire... I'll .." The draft board medical examiner looked at him and said, "Man, you're crazy!" to which the student replied, "Write that down! Write that down!"

(894)

At the end of a bitter argument, the husband roared, "I'm sick of you and your ways. I'm going out and get something I've never had before!" The wife replied, "If you had another two or three inches, you could get something HERE you never had before!

(895)

Did you hear about the sleepy bride who couldn't stay awake for a second?

(896)

The doctor told the rich man's young wife, "I have good news and bad news for you!" First the good news, "Your husband has an incurable disease and can't last longer than six months!" And now the bad news, "He got it from you!"

(897)

The doctor told the young man, "I've got good news and bad news for you!" The bad news is your leg is in such bad shape that I am going to have to cut it off!" The good news is "The man in the next bed wants to buy your boots!"

(898)

Asked by his teacher to spell "Straight," the third grade student rattled off the letters perfectly. "Now," said the teacher, "what does the word mean?" Replied the kid, "without water!"

(899)

A first grade teacher was in the lobby of a hotel where she was attending a teacher's convention. On her way to the elevator, she encountered a man whose face looked vaguely familiar from the many PTA meetings she had attended at her school. "I beg your pardon, Sir," she said rather timidly, "But aren't you the father of one of my children?" Quickly recovering from his initial surprise, the man tipped his hat, smiled and replied, "No Ma'am, but it would have been my pleasure!"

(900)

"Tell me honey," the man said to the pregnant woman with a large bulge, " are you going to have a baby?" "No," she said, "I'm just carrying it for a friend!"

(901)

I still have a lot of trouble with wrong numbers. Yesterday I dialed the Red Cross and got the Internal Revenue Service by mistake. So the IRS operator asked me what number I had dialed. I said, "The Red Cross... where they take your blood." She said," Well, you aren't too far off, are you?"

(902)

You have to watch out for little old ladies. Last week one of them came up to me and said, "Mr. O'Brien, you may find this hard to believe, but your speech reminded me of a little dog I have at home." I said, "Isn't that sweet! My speech reminded you of a little dog you have at home? What kind of dog? She said, "Bull!"

(903)

Let's never give up the two party system. If we crossed a donkey with an elephant, do you realize what we'd end up with? A jackass that never forgets!

(904)

Ladies, it is not necessary to tell your doctor everything about your private life! For instance, if he points his shot needle in your direction and says, "When I stick it in, you won't feel a thing," please don't acknowledge him by saying, "Ha, Ha, that reminds me of my husband!"

(905)

One day at the Peacock Lounge, Homer whispered to the bartender, "Do me a favor buddy, please spread the word around that I had a vasectomy!" The bartender replied, "Boy, you must be in real pain!" Homer said, "No, between you and me, the story is a big lie but when my wife hears the rumor, she will sure as hell be damn careful when she invites the mailman to come in."

(906)

Ever hear of the little Wisconsin town of "GOTITALLIN?" Know how it got its name? Well, this romantic Indian buck took a healthy young squaw for his new bride. She was a virgin, so he started out very slowly and carefully, just an inch at a time. After a few moments, the new bride started enjoying it and she started yelling, "More more more !" The groom looked down and said, "Can't give you anymore, Honey...got it all in!"

(907)

Do you know what goes up when it's warm and goes down when it cools off ? Oh, come on now, you know it's a hot air balloon!

(908)

Did you hear about the couple who met in a marriage counselor's office for an attempt at reconciliation? The husband said, "Look, we've both said and done things we shouldn't have. Let's forget about all that and go back to the way it was on our honeymoon. We'll go home and I'll make passionate love to you!" She said, "Over my dead body." He said, "That's right. That's the way it's been for years!"

(909)

Secretaries are devious. Mine came back from her vacation and said, "Would you like to see where I got sunburned?" I said, "I sure would." She showed me a picture postcard of Miami Beach!

(910)

The family physician told a woman patient, "By the way, you can tell your husband his secretary was in this morning and he has nothing to worry about!" She replied, "The hell he doesn't, I'm going home and shoot that S.O.B.!"

(911)

Fellows, smarten up! If your wife wakes up in the middle of the night and says, "If you want to honey, you can..." Don't say a word until she finishes the sentence. Three Saturday's in a row now, I've been tricked into taking out the garbage and mowing the lawn!

(912)

When you are invited to a wedding and a schedule conflict prevents you from going, don't waste your time sending the bride and groom your regrets... they will soon have more than enough of their own!

(913)

When you find a real funny story and you tell it to a friend, please don't use the term, "Do you get it?" ... Number one, it's none of your business, and two, people are trained not to screw and tell!

(914)

SUSPENSE is when the dentist tells you to open your mouth and the next thing you hear is a zipper going down!

(915)

Early to bed and early to rise can bring a man wisdom and wealth. But sex three times a night, if you are doing it right, can start to ruin your health!

(916)

The cute little coed asked her professor, "Is it possible for a girl to get a hard on?" The professor smiled and replied, "It sure is, honey. If you will stay after class, I will be happy to give you one!"

(917)

Homer & Hector were admiring a poster of a beautiful Hollywood sex symbol. Homer spoke up and said, "I understand she came from your hometown. Did you know her ?" Hector grinned and replied, "Did I know her? I gave that little girl something she had never had before." Homer's eyes opened wide and he said, "You don't mean?" Hector replied, "You should be ashamed of thinking the way you do, all I did was give her a good case of chicken pox!"

(918)

Did you hear about the dummy who put a small mattress and a pillow on top of his television set? His girlfriend was coming to his apartment for dinner and he knew, once dinner was over she would say, "What's good on television tonight?"

(919)

The head chef at Maneros Restaurant was being interviewed by the TV reporter. "Do you use many condiments?" He answered, "Nope, I don't use any at all. My wife is on the pill!"

(920)

Remember the one about the young girl who woke up one morning with an elephant laying beside her? The girl said, "Oh my God, I must have really been tight last night" to which the elephant replied, "Yes, you were, but only for a little while."

(921)

The young man was asking his future wife's father for permission to marry his daughter. The father told him, " I want you to give this some serious thought, I want you to know that my daughter has acute angina," to which the future groom, replied, "Yes sir, I already know that, and by the way, she has a set of beautiful tits, too!"

(922)

The physician informed the young man that his recent examination found that he was infected with AIDS. The doctor informed him, "According to the law, I am required to report your situation along with the names of your past fifty sex partners." "You have to be kidding, Doc!" yelled the young man. "Do you think I've got eyes in the back of my head!"

(923)

As long as I live, I will never forget "What's his name?"

(924)

Do you know the definition of "Mixed Emotions?" That's when you see your mother-in-law driving your new 1997 Cadillac over a 1,000 foot cliff !

(925)

A couple slept in separate bedrooms, and the man was awakened one night by his wife's screams. He rushed into her room and snapped on the light just in time to see a male figure disappearing through the window. "That man attacked me twice!" wailed the woman. "Then why didn't you yell sooner?" exclaimed her husband. "Because I thought it was you," she sobbed, "until he started to have seconds! "

(926)

An evangelist was delivering a flaming sermon on vice that shook the rafters of the mission. "Listen to me, all you cigarette suckers," he thundered, "all you pipe suckers, all you bottle suckers . . . " Just then a high squeaky voice interjected from the back row, "Don't forget about us!"

(927)

A man went to the hospital for a vasectomy. During the operation, the surgeon's scalpel slipped and severed a testicle, so he sent a nurse to the cafeteria for an onion, which he sutured in as a replacement. Some time later, the patient returned for his final checkup and the surgeon asked him how he felt. "Just fine," said the man, "except for three things. First, when I pee, my eyes water. Second, when we have intercourse, my wife complains of heartburn. And third, every time I pass a hamburger joint, I get a hard-on!"

(928)

Two hens were strolling across the barnyard. Suddenly one hen clucked, "Oh no, here comes that cross-eyed rooster! We'd better separate, or he'll miss us both!"

(929)

When the test results were in, the physician told the young woman she was pregnant. "Do you have any idea when it might have happened?" He questioned. The girl thought for a few moments before replying. "I'm really not sure, doctor," she finally murmured, "but it might have been one time about six weeks ago, when my boyfriend and I didn't have anything special to do and he suggested a game of strip poker. It could be I raised him once too often."

(930)

When the executive came home from work one evening, he found his small son sitting on the front steps, crying. The father asked what was wrong and the boy said, "That Mr. Cole next door is a mean man!" "Why?" the father inquired. "Because he brought Mommy some ice cream and didn't give me any!" sobbed the son.
"Ice cream" Are you sure it was ice cream. ?" asked the man.
"Sure, I'm sure," wailed the youngster, "cause I heard Mommy tell him to hurry up before it got soft."

(931)

A far-out inventor has come up with a vibrating tampon. He figures that if women are going to feel miserable every month, they might as well enjoy it.

(932)

It was in Montana that a teenage girl told her mother that she had caught a ride home from the rural school with an Indian brave who had let her ride behind him on his horse. The mother wanted to know how the girl had kept from falling off. "It was simple, Mom," she replied. "I just put my arms around the Indian and held onto his saddle horn."

The mother gazed long and fixedly at her daughter. "Indians," she finally said, "don't use saddles."

(933)

The couple was divorced but remained good friends. When the man happened to break his arm, he called up his ex-wife one night and asked if she could possibly come over to help him take a bath, and she readily agreed. After she had helped him into the tub and had begun washing his back, she noticed a change gradually take place in his anatomy. "Now, isn't that sweet," she cooed. "Look Harry, it still recognizes me!"

(934)

A campus biggie went out for the first time with the vivacious little baton twirling champion of the college marching band, and he ended up in the hospital. "What happened, Bob?" inquired his visiting roommate. "Let's call it a case of overreaction," groaned the patient. "After the dance and a hamburger, we drove over and parked in Memorial Grove. Matters proceeded nicely and she began to give me a tantalizingly slow hand job but then some jerk in the car alongside began to whistle the school fight song!"

(935)

Instead of giving your wife a mink coat, a diamond bracelet, or a sports car for Valentine's Day... give her a canary. Then, every time it opens its mouth, she'll think of you. Especially when it says, "CHEEP!"

(936)

Did you hear about the guy who got 40,000 <u>Men's Names</u> out of the phone book ? He sent them a Valentine card, doused in French perfume and signed "Guess Who?" You know what his profession is - a divorce lawyer!

(937)

The pro quarterback was petitioning the court to have his recent marriage annulled. "On what grounds?" questioned the judge. "Non-virginity," replied the quarterback "When I married her, I thought I was getting a tight end, but instead I found I've gotten a wide receiver."

(938)

The young man who had offered the girl a ride home after work proved to be as entertaining as he was handsome. Upon arriving at her door, she invited him up for a drink , one thing led to another and they spent a wonderful night together. But when the girl woke up, her companion had already dressed and left, and she realized that she knew little about him except his first name. Determined not to lose touch with such a charmer, she ransacked her memory and finally recalled that he had said that he worked on a game bird farm in the suburbs. So she checked the Yellow pages, telephoned the place and gave his first name and described him.

"Yeah," said the man on the phone, "That's Pete Morrell, lady. He's a pheasant plucker.'

"He sure is!" agreed the girl. "And he has a pleasant smile and personality, too."

(939)

A convention delegate was trying hard to get a package of cigarettes from a machine in the lobby. Suddenly the machine 'gave' and his elbow jammed right into the knocker of a good-looking girl who was passing by. Very embarrassed, he said to her, "If your heart is as soft as your breast dear, you will find room to forgive me." She smiled and said, "I forgive you, and if you have anything else as hard as your elbow, my room number is 669!"

(940)

The city boy was visiting his country cousin, who promptly took him down to the barn and proceeded to educate him in the country ways of making love to the cows. But as the city boy was in the middle of the operation, he appeared very disgusted, and remarked, "This doesn't do a thing for me," the country cousin replied, "Well, it 'taint no wonder... you picked the ugliest heifer in the bunch!"

(941)

The well endowed girl asked the bartender for a "Martooni" and was served. She had a second and a third. Then the bartender asked if she cared for another. "I don't like your Martoonis... they give me heartburn," she answered. And the bartender countered with, "For your information, lady, the name's not Matoonis, but Martinis, and you haven't got heartburn, your left knocker's in the ashtray!"

(942)

Jane and Elaine, sisters-in-law, were lunching together. Jane remarked, "I envy you, being married to a man who doesn't drink" Elaine asked, "What do you mean, doesn't drink? " Jane said "You've been married to my brother for years. Have you ever seen him touch a drop?" Elaine answered thoughtfully "No, and I guess he's never actually said he DID drink... but just wait till the next time he tells me he stopped off for a quick one !"

(943)

He was walking along the street and ran into an old girlfriend and said, "Hello, Jell-O!" She asked, "Why do you call me Jell-O?" and he said, "Because you're easy to make." So they made a date, and that night as he was leaving her house she said, "Goodbye, oatmeal!" He asked, "Why do you call me oatmeal ?" She laughed and answered, "Because you get hot and sticky and in three minutes you're done."

(944)

The lady's car got stuck in a mud hole on a country road, so she walked up to the farm house and asked the farmer to come pull her out. He came up on his tractor and she rode with him. On the way he remarked, "You're the third pregnant woman I've pulled out of the mudhole today." She said, "But I'm not pregnant," and he replied, "And you're not out of the mudhole yet, either."

(945)

Joe sat at his dying wife's bedside. Her voice was little more than a whisper. "Joe, darling," she breathed, "I've a confession to make before I go. I ... I'm the one who took the $10,000 from your safe ... I spent it on a fling with your best friend, Charles. And it was I who forced your mistress to leave the city. And I am the one who reported your income tax evasion to the government ... " "That's all right, dearest, don't give it a second thought," answered Joe. "I'm the one who poisoned you!"

(946)

"I've learned one thing about women," said the experienced one to his drinking companions. "You just can't trust a girl with brown eyes." "It occurs to me," said one of his inebriated friends, "that I've been married nearly three years and I don't know what color eyes my wife has." The second man finished his drink, climbed from his stool and hurried home to investigate this disturbing possibility. His wife was in bed asleep. He crept up to her and carefully lifted an eyelid.

"By God! *Brown!"* he exclaimed.

"How the hell did you know I was here?" said Brown, crawling out from under the bed!"

(947)

"That wife of mine is a liar," said the angry husband to a sympathetic pal seated next to him in the bar. "How do you know ?" the friend asked. "She didn't come home last night and when I asked her where she'd been, she said she had spent the night with her sister, Shirley." "So?" "She's a liar. I spent the night with her sister, Shirley!"

(948)

A young wife whose husband had grown neglectful decided that the best way to arouse his dormant interest would be to shock him into jealousy. "Darling," she purred one night, "the doctor I visited today said I had the most flawless face, full, well-rounded breasts and the loveliest legs he'd ever seen." "And did he say anything about your fat ass?" her husband asked her. "Oh no, dear," she said calmly, "your name wasn't mentioned once during our talk!"

(949)

Although he kept bachelors' hours, Harry quite piously demanded absolute fidelity from his wife. Almost every night he would leave her at home with the children, bidding her farewell with a cheery, "Goodnight, mother of three." Then one night she called back just as cheerfully, "Goodnight, father of one. " Now... Harry stays home every night!"

(950)

A gravedigger, thoroughly absorbed in his work, dug a pit so deep one afternoon that he couldn't climb out when he had finished. Come nightfall and evening's chill, his predicament became more uncomfortable. He shouted for help and at last attracted the attention of a drunk staggering by.

"Get me out of here," the digger pleaded. *"I'm cold!"*

The inebriated one peered into the open grave and finally spotted the shivering digger in the darkness.

"Well, no wonder you're cold, buddy," said the drunk, kicking some of the loose sod into the hole. "They forgot to cover you up!"

(951)

Homer hurried to church one morning to see his priest. "Father," he said excitedly, "I made love ten times last night!" "Homer, I'm surprised at you," the priest replied sternly. "Is the woman married?" "Oh yes, Father, she's my wife." "But you don't have to come to confession if you make love to your wife." "I know.......but, I was so proud, I had to tell somebody!"

(952)

The old bull's active days were over, but the kindly farmer permitted him to stay on in the pasture with the cows. Of course, the farmer also turned a young bull loose in the field and the newcomer went to work immediately. Seeing this, the old bull began snorting and pawing the ground with his hoof. "You're wasting your time," said the farmer. "You're too old for that sort of thing now." "I know," said the bull, "but I can show him I'm not a cow, can't I ?"

(953)

She had just finished her shower when the doorbell rang. Tip-toeing to the front door, shivering in plump, pink nudity, she called, "Who is it?" "The blind man," came a mournful voice, so she shrugged and opened the door with one hand while reaching for her purse with the other. When she turned to face the man, he was grinning from ear to ear, and she saw that he was holding a large package in his arms. "You can see!" she exclaimed. "Yeah," he nodded happily. "And mighty pretty, too. Now, where do you want I should put these blinds?"

(954)

"Why do you lower your eyes when I say I love you ?" , the young man asked the attractive girl in the nudist camp. "It's the only way I know whether or not you're telling the truth", she replied .

(955)

DID YOU HEAR ??? ... about the lady who visited a furniture store and asked to see a "sexual couch ?" The salesman, masking his amusement, politely asked, "Don't you perhaps mean a sectional couch, madam?" "No, no," she replied emphatically. "I'm sure my interior decorator told me I should have a sexual couch for an occasional piece in the living room."

(956)

While searching for and old Army buddy's apartment in a small town, a uniformed Vietnam veteran spotted two spinster ladies though a living room window and stepped up onto their porch to ask for directions. When one answered the door, the other inquired who their visitor was. "It's a young soldier and he's got a Purple Heart on," said the old lady at the door, looking the soldier up and down. "I don't care what color it is," came the voice inside. "Let him in."

(957)

Two ladies at the Old Folks Home were chatting, and one asked the other, "Tell me, Matilda Mae, if you could live your whole life over, what would you do different? " Matilda Mae replied, "I'd get me a husband who could screw as good as yours."

(958)

With his last will and testament completed, the old man in the oxygen tent fondly told his son that all his wealth, stocks, bonds, bank accounts and real estate would be his after the end finally came. "Dad, Dad," whispered the weeping son, his voice emotion-choked "I can't tell you how grateful I am. . . . how unworthy I am.... is there .... is there anything I can do for you ? Anything at all ? "Well, son," came the feeble reply, "I'd appreciate it very much if you took your foot off the oxygen hose."

(959)

The 80-year-old man was aging rapidly. "Your hearing is getting worse," announced his physician during a periodic check-up, "and you must cut out all smoking, drinking and sex." "What!" cried the fellow. "Just so I can hear a little better?"

(960)

It was midnight when the phone rang at police headquarters. The desk sergeant answered and a shrill voice reported, "There's a sex maniac in my house." "Try to be calm, lady," the cop said reassuringly. "We'll have a patrol car there in a few minutes." "Oh, that's not necessary," the caller chimed. "Just send somebody around to pick him up in the morning!"

(961)

"Senator," asked one of his aides during a working-luncheon . "What do you intend doing about the Abortion Bill?" "Shhh, not so loud," gulped the legislature. "Phone that quack and tell him I'll pay it first thing next month."

(962)

The old country doctor had been approached once too often by the town gossip, who wanted this time to know about Mrs. Brown's new baby. "The child was born without a penis," he said. "Oh!" gasped the woman. "But," added the doctor, "she'll have a damn nice place to put one in eighteen years!"

(963)

It's a "Damn Shame!" That's a bus load of convicted Child Molesters going off a 1,000 foot cliff and two of the seats are empty.

(964)

Before starting the Sunday sermon, Reverend Jones told his congregation, "It has come to our attention that someone in the flock is calling our piano player a mother fugger. I want to know who said it." A man in the back of the church raised his hand. The preacher shouted, "Why, Deacon Buchanan! Did you really call our piano player a mother fugger?" The deacon rose to his feet and retorted hotly, "I did not sir! I would just like to know who it was that called this mother fugger a piano player?"

(965)

GENERAL MISCELLANEOUS

It was a cold, miserable day in rural Minnesota when a traveling salesman got lost and stopped at a farm house for directions. After visiting for a while and noticing that the snow as 14 inches deep, the temperature around zero, he asked the farmer, "In this remote part of Minnesota, what do you people do for fun in the cold winter time ?" "Well," the farmer replied, "Mainly we hunt and screw." "Really... what do you hunt for?" "Usually," the farmer replied, "something to screw".

(966)

Did you hear about the college graduate who got his first big job with Coca-Cola in Atlanta? His starting salary was $100,000.00 per year. All he had to do was to call on ten women executives per week and *knock 7- Up!*

(967)

Telling people to abstain from sex is like singing "Oh, come all ye faithful" at a wife-swapping party!

(968)

The cute young girl told the little old man, "Mister, I am not that kind of girl! Also, Momma said I should never do it. Besides, the grass is wet and anyhow, ten dollars is not enough!"

(969)

Did you hear about the drunk screaming in the Men's Room at the local bar? The bartender and some of the patrons rush into the men's room. The drunk looked up and said, "Every time I flush this damn thing, it comes up and bites my balls!" "Of course it does," the bartender laughed, "You're sitting on the mop bucket!"

(970)

The doctor was giving a speech on medical research at the annual convention. "We have finally developed a replacement for that inconvenient daily birth control pill! We already have a morning after one, and I am sure it won't be long until some laboratory will come up with a pill to be taken only once per month." One of the doctors in the front row yelled up, "Are you kidding? With my wife, a monthly pill would be over-medication!"

(971)

I'm sure you have heard about the new breakfast cereal called "Queerios." All you do is add milk and they eat each other!

(972)

ANOTHER POEM:
Roses are red and Violets are blue
The hell with the foreplay, why don't we just screw!

(973)

Sadie told Helen Patricia, "I sure thought a lot about Homer, but he turned out to be a real disappointment." I went with him for over six months and he would continually tell me he could get it up higher and keep it up longer than any other man. I didn't know his hobby was flying kites!"

(974)

A young wife visited an obstetrician and said, "I think I'm pregnant." He smiled gently and asked, "How many times have you missed?" She replied, "Gosh, doctor, we haven't missed a night since we've been married."

(975)

AND ANOTHER TOAST...
Here's to my wife .. The light of my life ..
She fell asleep in just a minute, slept all night with my thing in it!

(976)

Hey guys, "pour our girlfriend the new *daylight savings cocktail.* Only one sip and she will spring forward and then fall back on her back !"

(977)

How do you figure it? If George Washington is the Father of our County, in spite of the fact that his wife, Martha had no children ... "What do you figure that makes you and I?"

(978)

A PERFECT GIFT FOR YOUR NEXT WEDDING
Make sure the bride and-groom have at least a dozen cream colored sheets for their bed!

(979)

Do you know what doctors say under their breath every time a new baby is born? As they pat its little butt, they say "Boy this kid has to be dumb .. Anyone who would crawl into a hole like that ought to be spanked! "

(980)

How about the smart doctor who collected all the skins he cut off patients who requested to be circumcised ? He saved them up until he had enough skin to make a billfold. What made them so unique was the fact that you could rub the wallet three or four times and it would turn into a suitcase.

(981)

Hilda answered the phone, "Hello, who is this?" On the other end of the line came the response, "This is Mike!" Hilda said, "Now wait a minute, let me guess, are you the Mike who screws so well, or the one who thinks I am still a virgin?"

(982)

I wouldn't say my girlfriend is dumb, but she absolutely will not use any face soap accept "Dial." When it is spelled backwards, it reminds her of the good time she is expecting tonight!

(983)

A letter to the "Preparation H" company:

Dear Sir:

You know those big pills you sell in all the drug stores? Well, I bought six boxes of them and for all the good they did me, I might as well have stuck them up my butt!

(984)

I bet you don't know what's hard, round, hairy at one end, and when a male uses it, his female is glad? Sure you know ??? It's just a shaving lather brush!

(985)

The corpse of a missing salesman was found with multiple stab wounds in the back, both hands and feet securely tied together. Judge Homer Chump has ruled it a suicide. By the way, the body was found under the bed of the wife of Judge Chump!

(986)

A husband was in the living room watching television. He yells to his wife in the kitchen, "Honey, come and watch this movie." She said, "Do you have a good one on?" Her husband replied, "If I did, we sure wouldn't waste time watching TV!"

(987)

Did you hear about the girl who said, "I will do anything for a mink coat!" When she got it, she couldn't button it!

(988)

A "Dialing for Dollars" disc jockey talking to a lady on the phone ...

"You can be our winner of $500 if you can answer the following question! The question is... "Who was the first man?" The lady replied, "I wouldn't tell you for a thousand dollars!"

(989)

Have you tried the new cocktail called "Span-Lax?" It's half Spanish Fly and half-melted Ex-Lax! If you drink three of them, I guarantee, you won't know whether you're coming or going!

(990)

After only one year of marriage, the young man came home and exclaimed to his Dad, "You know Dad, I think I married a Nun!" "What do you mean" says the old man. "Well," the son replied, "there is none in the morning, none at noon, none in the afternoon and none when we go to bed at night!" His Dad had a big grin on his face as he said, "Son, I want you to go into the kitchen right now and meet Mother Superior!"

(991)

You heard about Judy, the juvenile delinquent, who got kicked out of school only because they caught her doing pushups in an asparagus patch!

(992)

Did you hear about the old maid who saw a handsome fellow's picture in *a WANTED POSTER* at the Post Office? She told the Postmaster that she would pay one hundred dollars more than the F.B.I.

(993)

And then, there was the one about the three drunks who had died and were at the Gates of Heaven. They met St. Peter who had only one question before they were allowed inside the Pearly Gates ... "What happened to cause your death?" The first drunk said, "I died from Aids." St. Peter says, "Come on in!" The second drunk says, "I died from cancer." And again St. Peter says... "Come on in!" The third drunk said, "I died from seen-us." St. Peter says, "Come on now, you don't mean seen us, you mean SINUS!" "No," the third drunk says, "I really did die from seen-us. I was laying in the bed with a married woman and her husband 'SEEN US!"

(994)

How about the Fire Department called to a hotel fire? As one of the firemen started going up the steps with the hose, he encountered this drunk, pulling up the zipper of his fly. The drunk stopped the fireman and said "Hi Buddy, if you see a naked woman running around up there, go ahead and screw her, I have already paid for it!"

(995)

This Australian visiting America, took this call girl to his motel room and while she was undressing, the Australian started moving all the furniture to one side of the room. The call girl looked at him and said, "What the hell are you doing?" The Australian said, "Well, Ma'am, I've never done this with a girl before, but if it's anything like a kangaroo, we are going to need all the room we can get!"

(996)

How about the truck driver who picked up this hippie man on the highway. For the first fifteen minutes, neither of them said a word and all of a sudden the hippie said, "I guess you are trying to figure out, with my clothes and long hair, whether or not I am a boy or a girl!" The truck driver replied, "Makes no damn difference, you are going to get screwed anyway!"

(997)

Have you heard about the grade school teacher and what the kids did for her a couple of days prior to the end of the school year? One of the white students walked into his classroom and presented the teacher with a beautiful Angel Food cake. On top of the cake was inscribed, "T.O.T." The teacher expressed her appreciation and asked, "Honey, what's the T.O.T. Stand for?" The youngster replied, "TO OUR TEACHER." The next day, one of the black students came in the classroom with a large delicious looking chocolate cake and on top was inscribed, "F.U.C.K" Again, the teacher thanked them for thinking of her, but again had to ask... "What does the letters on top of the cake stand for?" The little colored boy said, "THAT'S EASY TEACHER, IT MEANS IT IS FROM US COLORED KIDS !"

(998)

Then, there was the football coach of this small town who had not won a football game all season. One of the merchants in town got him cornered one day and asked the questions, "Coach, what's the story?" He said, "Your team has played 12 games this year, they haven't even scored one touchdown and you have lost every game." The coach thought for a moment and then said, "Well, I really don't know, but I have a feeling that it was because I used an *unbalanced line* and, between you and me, those kids in the back field weren't too smart either."

(999)

Two wives talking over the back fence and one says, "My husband is impossible! He now insists on having sex once a week." The neighbor replied, "That doesn't sound unreasonable." "It does to me," said the first wife ... "he used to get it once a night!"

(1000)

The missionary was walking through the jungle with his new native friend. They saw a monkey and the missionary said, "Monkey." The native repeated "Monkey." They saw a parrot and the missionary said "Parrot," and the cannibal replied "Parrot." Then came a native man who was busy having sex with a native girl. The missionary thought fast and said "man on sled." The native again repeated what the missionary had said and immediately grabbed his spear and sunk it into the back end of the man on the girl. That was when the cannibal said "man on My sled!"

(1001)

YOU HAVE GOT TO BUY ONE OF THE NEW BUMPER STICKERS IT SAYS...
"SEX INSTRUCTOR - FIRST LESSON FREE"

(1002)

You got to go and you got to go NOW... how dry I am, how wet I'll be, if I don't find the bathroom key... I found the key, it was in the door, but I'm too late, it's on the floor!

(1003)

You will know when you getting old. It will be the day when you wake up with one of your legs across your wife and you ask yourself, "Was I getting on or off?"

(1004)

You know, with whiskey it's age, in a cigarette, it's taste and in a sports car, its damn near impossible!

(1005)

Did you hear about the drunk in the cemetery kneeling beside a grave, crying his eyes out and screaming, "Why did you die, oh why did you die?" A second drunk comes along and after watching and listening for a half hour to this guy saying, "Why did you die?", the second drunk had to ask, "say, ole buddy, I don't know who is buried here, but you must have loved them very much." 'NO," said the first drunk, "It's my wife's first husband, oh why did you die?"

(1006)

A sharp knock on the door startled the two lovers. "Quick, it's my husband! Jump out the window!" I can't do that, we are on the 13th floor! "JUMP!", said the woman. "THIS IS NO TIME TO BE SUPERSTITIOUS!"

(1007)

Today's modern used car salesman no longer tells his potential customer "this car was driven by a little old lady who used it only for church and grocery shopping." His story now is "This car was driven by a Nymphomaniac who used only the back seat."

(1008)

An Indian and a hippie were standing side by side in a bar. The Indian had been staring at the hippie for more than two hours. The hippie noticed and said, "Look Indian, get the hell out of here, you've been staring at me all afternoon." The Indian replied, "Yes sir, I have been looking at you. Many moons ago, me have sex with buffalo. I just wondered if you might possibly be my son!"

(1009)

The cute little lady was filling out an application for employment as a secretary. When she came to the blank marked 'Sex' she wrote, "Yes, for additional details, please read comments under SALARY REQUIRED!"

(1010)

Two drunks in the Peacock Lounge... one says to the other ..."Hey Buddy, I heard a rumor that your dad was getting married for the 5th time! Is there any truth to it?" The other drunk replied, "Hell no, it's not true, my father has never been married!"

(1011)

HAPPINESS IS:

Finding out your husband's secretary is knocked up and knowing that both you and he were out of the county on vacation when it happened.

(1012)

Do you know the definition of a birth control pill ? It's the other thing a woman can put in her mouth to keep from getting pregnant!"

(1013)

A TOAST FOR YOUR NEXT PARTY!
Here's to the girl of my dreams,
I could not ask for more
She's deaf and dumb and over sexed,
and owns a liquor store!

(1014)

Did you hear about the tourist and the camel ride in the South African desert? She got in the saddle, but the camel refused to get up on all fours. After about five minutes, her guide went inside the tent and came out with two bricks. He went to the rear of the camel, with a brick in each hand, and whacked the camel in the "balls." The camel immediately stood up and was ready to go. The tourist was shaking her head and told the guide, "Well, your bricks sure worked, but I would bet that really hurt like hell!" To which the guide replied, "No, not if you don't get your fingers between the bricks."

(1015)

Two drunks at the bar and one said, "You know, Joe, I have a problem! When my wife and I have sex, I never know really how far to stick it in!" Joe replied, "At one time I had the same problem, but I finally figured it out. When we have sex now, I simply put a piece of chewing gum on the end of it, when she starts chewing, I stop pushing!"

(1016)

And then, there was the one about the two old maids who went to the movie. They weren't there over a half hour till one old maid says to the other, "Helen Patricia, I don't know what to do! The man sitting beside me is masturbating." Helen Patricia replied, "We don't have to take this humiliation, let's get up and move." The first old maid said, "I can't, he's using my hand."

(1017)

The NBC reporter was interviewing the American astronaut, upon his return from Mars. The reporter asked, "What about the inhabitants on Mars, how do they compare with us humans on earth?" "Well," said the astronaut, "the people on Mars look almost the same as people on earth, the only difference is that the women have their breasts on their backs!" "Gosh," said the reporter, "I bet they sure are ugly!" "Not really," replied the astronaut, "It might hurt their looks a little bit, but it sure makes them a lot more fun to dance with!"

(1018)

HERE'S A TOAST FOR YOUR NEXT WEDDING PARTY
Here's to the health of the groom,
and here's to the health of the bride,
here's to their children especially,
The one her wedding dress can't hide!

(1019)

I'm sure you have heard about the couple on the stalled elevator who got off between floors!

(1020)

Then, there was the drunk who had his head down on the bar and was crying his heart out! The bartender noticed and asked, "What's the problem, mister?" "It's so embarrassing," mumbled the drink, "for a man to be arrested for indecent exposure and then be released for insufficient evidence!"

(1021)

CUTE LITTLE LOLITA...
She doesn't drink, she doesn't pet, she doesn't even go to grade school yet!

(1022)

Have you heard about the three buddies that really got drunk? One of the guys was an undertaker. Of the three, the undertaker and his buddy were in better shape than "Old Bill." Old Bill was completely passed out. To have fun, they picked up Old Bill and took him to the funeral home and placed him in an empty casket. The next morning, when Old Bill woke up with a splitting headache, he noticed his surroundings, tuned completely white and said, "God, what's going on? If I am alive, what in the hell am I doing in this casket? And, if I am dead, how come I have to pee so bad?"

(1023)

Then there is that new Rock and Roll song: "Hey Baby, won't you take a chance? I left my condom in my other pants!"

(1024)

Do you know what a Grasshopper is?
That's a guy who can't afford a motel!

(1025)

The birch tree and the beech tree were discussing their ancestry and the ancestry of a little tree up on a hill. They talked to a woodpecker about it and he remarked, "I really don't know if that little young sprout is a son-of-a-birch, or a son-of-a-beech, but I can tell you this, his mother was the most tender piece of ash I ever punched my pecker into!"

(1026)

The drunk walked up to the mounted Policeman and stuck his finger in the back end of the horse. The Policeman looked around and said, "Hey Buddy, what the hell do you think you are doing." "My buddy in that bar over there is bad sick and I'm trying to get him to throw up!" "For God's sake" replied the Policeman, "that's not going to get him to throw up!" "The hell it won't," said the drunk," when I take this finger out of the horse and put in my buddy's mouth, I guarantee you, he'll throw up!"

(1027)

Then there was the one about the drunk who got his finger smashed by the men's room door. He was taken immediately to the doctor who bandaged up the finger and gave him an antibiotic shot. "Doctor," moaned the drunk "when my finger heals, will I be able to play the piano?" "Of course you will," assured the doctor "Your a wonderful doctor," said the drunk "but I couldn't play the piano before! "

(1028)

During her annual checkup, the well-constructed miss was asked to disrobe and climb onto the examining table. "Doctor," she replied shyly, "I just can't undress right in front of you." "All right," said the physician, "I'll flick off the lights. You undress and tell me when you're through." In a few moments, her voice rang out in the darkness: "Doctor, I've undressed. What should I do with my clothes?" "Your clothes?" answered the doctor. "Put them over here, on top of mine."

(1029)

A 96-year-old man married an 84-year-old woman. Instead of saying "I do," he mumbled weakly, "I can only try!"

(1030)

You will know when you are in your "Twilight Years" That's when thoughts turn from passion to pension!

(1031)

A girl can take her first sex lesson lying down, but a boy is forced to learn it the hard way!

(1032)

Lipstick is a lovely gift, every wife reports... unless her hubby brings it home underneath his shorts!

(1033)

On the wall in Kellie's apartment is a sign that reads, "Push button for birth control." Her date for the evening pushed the button...and Kellie's mother came in with a shotgun! The little old lady asked the little boy, "Do you kiss your auntie when she comes?" The little boy replied, "No, but my uncle does!"

(1034)

The young boy, trying to make heads or tails out of his big brother's anatomy textbook, asked "Daddy, where are your testicles?" The father, with his head buried in the newspaper replied, "I don't know Son, ask your Mother ... she's the one who puts everything away and then can't find anything!"

(1035)

The husband and wife got bored with the same old routine every night, so they decided to try it with her on top. They enjoyed it so well they kept it up for a couple of months. Then one night, her husband insisted that they return to the normal or regular position. His wife was disappointed and said, "Didn't you like it with me on top?" He replied, "Yes, hon., I really loved it, but my boss told me today if I screw up one more time, I'm going to be looking for a new job!"

(1036)

I'm not much for cigars, but the other morning I went to the office with one in my mouth and asked my secretary if the cigar in my mouth made me look distinguished? She said, "it sure does, it makes you look like a movie star... the only way to describe it is Lassie, taking a crap!"

(1037)

Donna looked at Kellie's swollen stomach and said, "Oh baby, you are really getting fat!" Kellie smiled, "Yes, but this fat's the screwed on kind! Your big butt comes from eating too much!"

(1038)

Did you ever stop to think "How true it is!" Every mother in the world hopes her daughter will land a better man than she got, but she knows her son will never find a woman as good as his dad did!

(1039)

This egotistical male, after a satisfying "romp in the hay" with the prostitute, got out of bed, paid the girl and to be polite he said, "Is there anything else I can do for you before I leave?" The prostitute replied, "Yes, as a matter of fact, there is something more you can do for me... I would sure love to have your home address so I can send your wife a sympathy card."

(1040)

The college football player was out driving with the cute little cheerleader and told her, "There are only two traffic signs I respect. #1 is 'Soft Shoulders,' and the other one is 'Yield Right Away!'

(1041)

Do you know how to describe a "Hippie?" That's a guy who thinks he is Tarzan, looks like Jane, and smells like Cheeta!

Did you hear about the guy who walked into the bar a told the bartender, "I want 12 Martinis!" The bartender replied, "Boy, that is quite an order. You must be celebrating something!" The guy said, "Hell yes, I'm celebrating, I just had my first blow job!" The bartender again replied, "That is something... you have a right to celebrate. I'll tell you what, I'll just set up 13 Martinis for you and the last one will be on the house!" The guy said, "No, don't do that.. if 12 of the damn things don't take the taste out of my mouth, one more won't make any difference."

"Mommy, what's that between little brother's legs," asked little Daisy. "that's just his whistle, Dear," answered Mommy. A few hours later, after they had naps, Daisy spoke up and said, "Mommy, I blew Ferdie's whistle, but I couldn't get it to work!"

Crowded morning in the family bath. Little Mary, aged 6 and Johnny, 7, bathing together before school. Mary noted John's little dingo and said, "Mommy, I want one of those." And Mommy answered, "Be patient, Dear . . be a good girl and you'll have one when you grow up." And the Old Man spoke up through his shaving soap, "Yeah, and if you're a BAD little girl you'll get lots of them!"

LADY 1:   I'm sure mad at you!
LADY 2:   WHY?
LADY 1:   You've been going around telling people MY husband has a wart on the end of his apparatus!
LADY 2:   I never said that ... I only said it FELT like it!

(1046)

"You say this breaking out all over me is caused by worrying too much? Well, you're probably right, doctor... I do worry too much. I worry about my wife... I'm afraid she'll quit me for another man." The doctor laughed jovially and said to the patient, "So what if she does leave you, there are plenty of other fish in the sea." And the patient answered, "Maybe so, Doc, but my bait ain't what it used to be."

(1047)

The traveling salesman, selling to farmers, noticed in the barnyard a rooster dressed in pants, shirt and suspenders, and nearly died laughing. "We had a fire and he got all his feathers singed off," said the farmer, "So Ma made him some clothes to keep him warm. If you think he LOOKS funny, you should see him holding down an old hen with one foot, and trying to get his pants down with the other!"

(1048)

Then, there was the young preacher who was working on a crossword puzzle and asked the older preacher, "What is a four-letter word that ends in "T" and it describes a woman?" The older pastor thought for a moment and replied, "That's easy. The word is 'Aunt'." "Well, I'll be darned," said the young pastor, "By the way, my dear friend, you don't have an eraser on you, do you?"

(1049)

In a tender moment, a woman told her husband, "You're the best lay in this whole town!" Instead of thanking her, he bellered, "How come YOU know?" Without missing a stroke, she said, "Your secretary told me."

(1050)

The school bus driver needs nerves of steel and a poker face so as not to laugh when some kid inquires, "Will you let me and my brother Jack off now?"

(1051)

The aging scoundrel told his new housekeeper, "I'm a man of few words. If I pinch your bosom, that means "Come to bed." She said, "that suits me fine, as I'm a woman of few words myself. If I crack your skull with a skillet, it means I'm not coming!"

(1052)

A father, entering his son in college, introduced himself and the lad to the school's president, thusly: "I'm Mr. Bates, and my son, Master Bates." The school man replied, "Don't apologize sir... most of the boys here do that."

(1053)

EPITAPH
Here lies a good man
Beside his good wife.
Believe if you can:
They lived without strife.
The reason is plain,
They abounded in riches;
Had no care nor pain
And wife wore the britches!

(1054)

When Jack told Jill he was breaking their engagement to marry someone else, Jill asked, "Can she cook gourmet foods like I can?" Jack said, "No." Jill demanded, "Can she buy you anything you want like I can?" Again Jack, said, "No." Jill pleaded tearfully, "Can she make love as well as I?" A sad look came over Jack's face, and he shook his head no. Jill shrieked, "Well, what in hell CAN she do?" Jack replied, "I hate to tell you honey, but she is going to sue me for child support!"

(1055)

A man and his wife was having a cocktail before dinner when the phone rang. The wife was closest, so she picked up the phone. Before she could say anything, a man's voice came in loud and clear, "Honey, I won't be home for a while yet....I'm still working at the office." The husband heard, grabbed the phone before his wife could say anything and said, "That's all right, old buddy, don't be in any hurry." Then hung up.

(1056)

If you have a happy hour at your home, here is some advice ... Never spoil good whiskey with water. Think of all the fish that had sexual intercourse in it!

(1057)

DEAR OLD DAD
My father was a gentleman,
And musical to boot.
He used to play piano
In a house of ill repute.
The Madame was a lady,
And a credit to her cult.
She enjoyed my Pappy's playing,
and I was the result!

(1058)

A Rabbi and a Priest accidentally walked into a gay bar to have a drink. Before long, a young man approached the Priest. "May I have the next dance?" he asked. The Priest was aghast, flustered and speechless. He turned to the Rabbi and mumbled, "Help me out of this. I'm so embarrassed." The Rabbi whispered into the gay man's ear and the young fellow immediately strode away. The Priest sighed in relief. "Herb, thanks a million! What in the world did you tell him?" "That we're on our honeymoon!"

(1059)

There are three men in every woman's life. The delivery man says, "Here it is... where do you want it?" The telephone man says, "Now that it's in, how do you like it?" And the dentist asks, "Now that it's out, how did it feel?"

(1060)

THE SENIOR CITIZEN LYRICS
FOR
SEPTEMBER SONG
Oh, it's a long, long while,
From June to October,
And we'd never have wed,
If I had been sober...
For my thing's dwindled down,
Till it's almost nil.
Yes, it's hard to get hard
When you're over the hill!

(1061)

A passenger noticed the bus driver was smiling a lot, so he asked, "Why are you so happy?" The driver said, "Me and my wife had a fight, and she cut me off for a month." The man asked, "Is that something to smile about?" The driver chirped, "It sure is... she don't even know where I'm getting it!"

(1062)

You know your kid's ugly when a talent scout for a model agency wants to use its face in a TV birth control commercial!

(1063)

Joe came home from the bar with a turkey, and his wife asked him how he got it. He said, "Oh, they had a contest down at the bar, and they gave a turkey to the one with the longest tool." His wife yelled, "You didn't haul ALL that thing out down at the bar, did you?" He replied, "No, just enough to win the turkey!"

(1064)

A young woman went to the doctor's office and told him she had a discharge. He told her to undress and get on the table. "Now," he said, "Spread your legs," and he started checking her. After a while, he asked, "How does that feel?" She said, "It feels WONDERFUL, but the discharge is in my ear!"

(1065)

A TOAST FOR YOUR LADY!

This toast should be recited while clinking glasses together, first at the bottom, then the top, and then the center of the glasses. You say: "Here's to my bottom, my top and my middle. Come with me honey, and I'll give you a little."

(1066)

GUESS T'WAT WE MEAN
It's lovely to look at,
and fondle as well.
But after much use
it still feels swell!

(1067)

An accountant suddenly up and married the woman he'd been living with for several years. His partner groaned, "That doesn't add up. I'd never buy a cow when I could get her milk and butter free." The groom rejoined, "You would if that cow was fixing to give you a calf! "

(1068)

The seventy-year-old man was delighted when his doctor told him his young bride was pregnant. "Doctor," he said, "That's wonderful news! Do you think I can do it again?" The doctor said, "Do you think you did it the first time?"

(1069)

THE PROBLEM WITH SEX

A dillar, a dollar,
A ten o'clock scholar,
What makes you come so soon?
If you wouldn't hump so fast,
We'd make it last till noon!

(1070)

"I'm sorry," the guy says to his girlfriend over the phone, "but I have to cancel our date tonight. I mashed my finger at work " The whole finger?" "No, the one next to the hole finger."

(1071)

What were the first words Adam spoke to Eve?
Stand back,! I don't know how big this thing gets!

1072)

Two dumb blondes were in a parking lot trying to unlock the door of their Mercedes with a coat hanger. They tried and tried to get the door open. The girl with the coat hanger stopped for a moment to catch her breath, and her friend said, "Hurry up! It's starting to rain and the top is down!"

(1073)

THE HAREY END

I had a little rabbit,
His fur was white as snow.
When my rabbit came of age,
He would not take it slow.
He hopped all day,
He hopped all night.
I remember how I cried.
He had the length,
But not the strength,
So my poor little bunny died!

(1074)

A TOAST FOR YOUR NEXT DATE...

Some men drink to actresses, some drink to sweethearts fair, but I drink to your pretty hair, may it never know a care. Virtue is an honor possessed by very few. But honey, you shouldn't be out with me... if you didn't plan to screw!

(1075)

Two young coeds took their 86-year-old Grandma out to lunch. It was a very hot day and the only parking place was in the sun. They were in the restaurant for about an hour, and when they came out, the leather car seats were burning hot. Grandma sat down and quickly remarked, "Gosh, I wish your Grandpa was here...my butt hasn't been this hot since our honeymoon!"

(1076)

Pregnant Polly had just told her folks she didn't know whose it was. Her dad suggested, "Pick the one who'll make the best husband. We'll pin it on him." Polly pondered, "Number 1 is richest. Number 2 loves me most, and Number 3 makes it best. But I guess I'll marry Wilfred." The father spluttered, "You're giving up money, love and sex for that bum Wilfred. It doesn't make sense." The little mother signed, "I know Daddy, but it's against the law to marry your brother, uncle or grandpaw!"

(1077)

ANOTHER TOAST
"Here's to my big thing,
and to your little thing, and
all things great or small.
If my big thing
got your little thing
we would have a ball!

(1078)

The old man came home and Johnny asked, "Daddy, can you go to heaven with your feet in the air?" and the old man said, "I don't know, son, why?" So Johnny explained, "Well, I came home and Ma was laying on the floor with her feet in the air hollering, "Holy Jesus, I'm coming," and she MIGHT have, if Uncle Bud hadn't been holding her down"

(1079)

NEWSPAPER WANT AD:
"Wish to purchase engine for 1948 Ford, or will sell body for $100."
Phone
Helen Hottail at 965-8973!

(1080)

Two neighbors were talking over the back, fence. "Bill, can I ask you a personal question?" "Tell me truthfully, how do you have sex most often?" His neighbor looked around to make sure his wife was not in hearing distance and said, "ALWAYS UNDER AN' ASSUMED NAME!"

(1081)

SIGN IN THE LADIES ROOM

"I wish I may, I wish I might,
Have a man in bed with me tonight,
Cause I'm so hot, but what the hell,
This toilet stool ain't no wishing well.
The urge is urgent, I just can't linger,
Look out below, here comes my finger!"

(1082)

After spending an afternoon on a muddy golf course, Dad decided to clean up his golf balls at the kitchen sink. Just then the telephone rang and his little 5-year-old daughter answered it. Hearing no more conversation in the adjoining room, the father asked "Who was it, honey?" She answered, "It was a lady Dad, but she hung up without leaving a message as soon as I told her you were in the kitchen washing your balls with a toothbrush." I still wonder which one of my wives friends was on the phone... ?

(1083)

HAVE YOU HEARD ABOUT THE NEW BOOK TITLED
"SCREAM IN THE NIGHT"
BY I.C. FINGERS

(1084)

WHAT DID THE PROSTITUTE SAY TO THE 80-YEAR OLD
MAN? "It'll have to be a quickie...at your age, too many strokes could
be fatal!

(1085)

The little boy offered to take an old lady's cocker for a walk. She
said, "All right, but don't let any other dogs whisper sweet nothings in
her ear." When he brought the puppy back, she asked, "Did any bad
dogs try to whisper in her ear?" The kid answered, "No, but one old
hound took out a little red pencil and wrote something under her tail!"

(1086)

An old man woke up on his 100th birthday and sat nude on the
edge of his bed. He looked at his hands and said, "Hands, you are one
hundred years old today." He looked at his legs and said, "Legs, you
are one hundred years old today." He looked at his penis and said,
"Well, old buddy, if you had lived, you would have been one hundred
years old today."

(1087)

The Mormon had nine wives. Eight of them had it pretty soft!

(1088)

The young groom had a strong feeling that his marriage wouldn't last when he asked his new bride, "Are you going to let me have some?" She answered, "Some what?"

(1089)

A mother told her 12 year old son, "Your Dad and I won't be home tonight. Do you want to sleep alone or with a baby sitter?" The young man looked at his Dad and said, "What would you do, Pop?"

(1090)

Did you hear about the rape at a Kentucky Truck Stop? This trucker was caught by the police for raping this waitress in the cab of his truck. In the courtroom, the Judge asked, "Do we have any witnesses to this crime?" Three truck drivers, on the scene, at the time, raised their hands. The Judge called up the first driver and asked, "What did you actually see?" The first trucker replied, "Well, your Honor, I looked in the truck cab and they were fucking!" The Judge hotly replied, "Now, wait a minute, we don't use those kind of words in the courtroom! You can use the word "sex" or "intercourse" but you don't use the word "fucking"! I am going to cite you for Contempt of Court and fine you ten dollars!" The Judge then continues, "Let us have the second witness now." The other trucker took the stand and the Judge again asked, "What did you see?" The second trucker said, "I saw the same thing as the first witness, I looked in the cab window and they were "fuckin !" Without any hesitation, the Judge again said, "I just informed you we don't use that word in the courtroom. I am also citing you and it's going to cost you 10 dollars!" Finally, the third trucker came up to the stand and told the Judge, "Well your Honor, there were ten toes up and ten toes down, two A-holes going around and around, six inches out and six inches in ... Now, if that's not "fuckin", here's my ten!"

Then there was this Rabbi who had just graduated from Rabbinical School. He called the sexton or janitor of the temple into his office and told him that he had a problem. He had never experienced sex and he knew that many of the younger members of the temple might ask him some questions regarding marital relations. He felt that, just once, he should experience "sex" so he would be in a position to answer any questions that he might encounter. The Sexton said "No problem Rabbi, there is a whore house just two blocks from the Temple; you go down there and I will make a phone call and get it all arranged." The new Rabbi arrived at the house and was met by this beautiful red head. She told the Rabbi that she had received a phone call and everything was arranged, please come upstairs to my bedroom. The red head asked the Rabbi, "Do you want to do it with the lights on or the lights off?" The Rabbi thought a moment and said, "Since this will be my first and last time, I might as well enjoy it to the best of my ability. Why don't we do it with the lights on?" She immediately started taking off her clothes and the Rabbi did the same. All of a sudden the red head looked at the Rabbi's penis and it was 24 inches long and at least 4 inches around. The red head immediately started putting her clothes back on as she told the new Rabbi, "I'm so sorry, but there is no way I can handle anything that big. You would ruin me and I would be out of business." With that, the Rabbi put his clothes back on and returned to the Temple to tell the Sexton what had happened. The Sexton said he was sorry and that he had called the wrong girl. "You go back down to the whore house and I will make another phone call." This time, the Rabbi was met at the front door by a gorgeous blonde. As they were going up the stairs, the blonde asked, "Rabbi, do you want to do it with the lights on or off?" Thinking what had happened before, the Rabbi informed her that he would like it with the lights off. They both got undressed; got into bed and in the proper position with the Rabbi on top of the blonde. Just then, the blonde looked into the Rabbi's eyes and said "You know Rabbi, I have always wondered, why don't the Jews believe in
JESUS CHRIST!!!"

How about the traveling salesman who was driving through the country side one day and came upon the three-legged chicken running right beside his car. The faster the car goes, the faster the chicken runs as he passes the salesman and runs up this lane to a farm. The salesman was amazed and decided to follow the chicken up the lane. There he encountered a farmer standing on the back porch. The salesman stopped his car, got out and walked up to the farmer. The salesman said, "I sure want to congratulate you, you must be a scientific genius to come up with a three-legged chicken. What was your reasoning?" The farmer replied, "Well, this is my business and I realized if I could grow a three-legged chicken, I could increase my profits by at least one-third." The salesman stood there with his mouth wide open and said, "That's a great idea, but I was wondering, "How do they compare to regular fried chicken?" The farmer replied, "Hell, I don't know, I can't catch the damn things!".

The little 5-year-old boy went to church with his dog one Sunday, tied the dog to a bush and walked up the church steps to encounter this 82-year-old lady.

OLD LADY: My, what a cute little boy ... you are so nice looking.
LITTLE BOY: Thank you ma'am!
OLD LADY: And look at that little blue blazer, white pants and a pretty tie, you are sure a good-looking boy!
LITTLE BOY: Thank you ma'am!
OLD LADY: And I see you have a cute little dog out there by the bush.
LITTLE BOY: Thank you ma'am!
OLD LADY: Honey, what do you call your dog?
LITTLE BOY: I calls him "Porkey"
OLD LADY: How come you call him Porkey?
LITTLE BOY: Cause he likes to screw pigs!!!

(1094)

The Police Officer stopped the drunk driving the wrong way on a one-way street. "Where the hell are you going?" asked the officer. The drunk replied, "Well, I was going to a party, but I must be too late. From the number of cars I've counted, everybody must have left!"

(1095)

Another drunk, going the wrong way on a one-way street was stopped by a cop who asked, "Hey Buddy, didn't you see those arrows?" The drunk studied for a moment and replied, "Hell no, I didn't even see the Indians!"

(1096)

Did you hear about the 18-year-old virgin man who was going to get married? He went to one of his friends to advise him what to do and, how to do it, when he took his new bride to the motel after the wedding. His friend told him the only way he could help him would be for him to occupy the room next door at the motel as he would have his ear on top the wall and would be able to answer any questions he might have. Everything went great at the wedding and the bride and groom took off for the motel. Upon arrival, the groom decided he needed to relieve himself in the bathroom. His bride undressed and got into bed when she had a violent urge to also go to the bathroom. She didn't want to hurry the groom, so she decided that she had the box her new bridal shoes came in, she would do it in the box When she was finished, she slid the box under the bed and just then the groom finally came out of the bathroom. Completely exhausted, he fell into bed and his hand fell off the side, directly into the shoe box. He raised his hand, looked at it for a second and then said, "My God! There's crap in the box!" His friend in the next room yelled, "Turn her over! Turn her over."

Here is one you and your wife or girlfriend can have fun with at your next party! It's the story of the little chicken who went to its mother one day to ask the question, "Where do I come from?" The wife plays the role of the baby chicken and the husband plays the role of the mother chicken ...

WIFE:	Mama, where did I come from? Am I people?
HUSBAND:	No sweetheart, you are a chicken.
WIFE:	Do chickens come from people?
HUSBAND:	No sweetheart, chickens come from eggs.
WIFE:	Are eggs born?
HUSBAND:	No honey, eggs are laid!
WIFE:	Are people laid?
HUSBAND:	Some sweetheart, the rest are chicken!!!

FRIEND:	Hi Homer. How long have you been married?
HOMER:	Six weeks.
FRIEND:	How's your love life? I bet you average three times a day!
HOMER:	No! To tell you the truth, my love life is not so good. All of a sudden my wife cut me down to only once a week!
FRIEND:	You're lucky! I know two guys she cut out all together!!

TO MY DEAR WIFE ...
"THE STORY OF OUR SEX LIFE!"

During the last year, I have tried to make love to you 365 times; I have succeeded 36 times, which is an average of about once every ten days. The following is a list of why I did not succeed more often.

- 54 times the sheets were clean
- 17 times it was too late
- 49 times you were too tired
- 15 times it was too hot
- 15 times you pretended to be asleep
- 3   times you said the neighbors would hear us
- 22 times you had a headache
- 7   times you were sunburned
- 9   times you said your mother would hear us
- 43 times you weren't in the mood
- 17 times you were afraid of waking the baby
- 6   times you were watching the late show on TV
- 6   times you didn't want to mess up your hair
- 15 times you said you were too sore
- 12 times it was the wrong time of the month
- 19 times you had to get up too early

Of those 36 times I did succeed, the activity was not satisfactory because 6 times you just laid there, 8 times you reminded me there was a crack in the ceiling, 4 times you told me to hurry up and get it over with, 7 times I had to wake you and tell you I had finished and once I was afraid I hurt you because I felt you move.

(Turn to next page for reply from Wife)

TO MY DEAR HUSBAND ...
"THE TRUE STORY OF OUR SEX LIFE"

I think you had things a little confused. Here are the real reasons you did not get more than you did!

- 5   times you came home drunk and tried to screw the cat
- 36 times you didn't come home at all
- 21 times you didn't come
- 33 times you came too soon
- 19 times you went soft before you got it in
- 10 times your toes were in a cramp
- 38 times you worked too late
- 29 times you had to get up early and play golf
- 2   times you were in a fight and got kicked in the balls
- 4   times you had a cold and nose kept running
- 3   times your coffee was too hot and you burned your tongue
- 2   times you had a splinter in your finger
- 20 times you lost the notion after thinking about it all day
- 6   times you came in your pajamas while reading RIS-K
- 98 times you were busy watching football on TV

Of the times we did get together, the reasons I laid still was because you missed and were screwing sheets. I wasn't talking about the crack, in the ceiling ... What I said was "Would you prefer me on my back, or kneeling?" The time you felt me move was because you farted and I was trying to breathe.

Your true Horoscope for this year !

AQUARIUS (Jan. 20 - Feb. 18) You have an inventive mind and are inclined to be progressive. You lie a great deal. On the other hand, inclined to be careless and impractical , causing you to make the same mistakes over and over again. People think you are stupid.

PISCES (Feb. 19 - Mar. 20) You have a vivid imagination and often think you are being followed by the CIA or FBI. You have minor influence over your associates and people resent you for your flaunting of your power. You lack confidence and are generally a coward. Pisces people do terrible things to small animals.

ARIES (Mar. 21 - April 19) You are the pioneer type and hold most people in contempt. You are quick tempered, impatient, and scornful of advice. You are not very nice.

TAURUS (April 20 - May 20) You are practical and persistent. You have a dogged determination and work like hell. Most people think you are stubborn and bull-headed . Taurus people have B.O.

GEMINI (May 21- June 20) You are a quick and intelligent thinker. People like you because you are bisexual. However, you are inclined to expect too much for too little. This means you are cheap. Gemini's are known for committing incest.

CANCER (June 21 - July 22) You are sympathetic and understanding to other peoples' problems. They think you are a sucker. You are always putting things off. That's why you'll never make anything of yourself. Most welfare recipients are cancer people.

(Continued next page)

LEO (July 23 - Aug. 22) You consider yourself a born leader. Others think you are pushy. Most Leo people are bullies. You are vain and dislike honest criticism. Your arrogance is disgusting . Leo people are thieves.

VIRGO (Aug. 23 - Sept. 22) You are the logical type and hate disorder. This nit-picking is sickening to your friends. You are cold and unemotional and sometimes fall asleep while making love. Virgo's make good bus drivers.

LIBRA (Sept. 23 - Oct. 22) You are the artistic type and have a difficult time with reality. If you are a man you are more than likely a queer. Chances for employment and monetary gains are excellent. Most Libra women are good prostitutes.

SCORPIO (Oct. 23 - Nov. 21) You are shrewd in business and cannot be trusted. You will achieve the pinnacle of success because of your total lack of ethics. Most Scorpio's people are murdered.

SAGITTARIUS (Nov. 22 - Dec. 21) You are optimistic and enthusiastic. You have a reckless tendency to rely on luck since you lack talent. The majority of Sagittarians are drunks or dope fiends. People laugh at you a great deal.

CAPRICORN (Dec. 22 - Jan. 19) You are conservative and afraid of taking risks. You don't do much of anything and are lazy. There has never been a Capricorn of any importance. Capricorns should avoid standing still too long as a dog might think you are a tree.

THIS IS THE VERY LAST PAGE

RETURN FROM AN EGO TRIP

Sometime, when you're feeling important,
Sometime, when your ego's in bloom,
Sometime, when you take it for granted
You're the best qualified in the room,
Sometime when you feel that your going
Would leave an unfillable hole,
Just follow this simple instruction,
And see how it. humbles your soul.

Take a bucket and fill it with water,
Put your hand in it up to the wrist;
Pull it out and the hole that's remaining
Is a measure of how you'll be missed.

The moral in this quaint example
is do just the best that you can,
Be proud of yourself, but remember,
There is no indispensable woman or man.

There you have it. "That's ALL FOLKS!" If you have enjoyed this book and
it has brought you a lot of laughs, be sure and tell your friends! If you didn't
like the book, please don't say a word!